Is Bobby Home?

BY BOB CIAMPITTI

DORRANCE
PUBLISHING CO
EST. 1920
PITTSBURGH, PENNSYLVANIA 15238

Dorrance Publishing Co
585 Alpha Drive
Pittsburgh, PA 15238
Visit our website at *www.dorrancebookstore.com*

ISBN: 979-8-89027-270-6
eISBN: 979-8-89027-768-8

Is Bobby Home?

THE TRUE LIGHT HEARTED ADVENTURES OF A BOY LIVING ON THE INNER-CITY STREETS OF PHILADELPHIA DURING THE 1950'S, AND 60'S

TAG ALONG AS THIS BOY, THINKING HE CAN DO ANYTHING, GETS HIMSELF AND HIS FRIENDS IN AND OUT OF CHILDHOOD SITUATIONS

THE ADVENURE BEGINS HERE

The year is 1954, Bobby lives in a small row home on a typical street in South Philadelphia. He is the younger of two boys born to second generation Italian immigrants in a neighborhood of similar families, mostly of Italian descent and a mixture of a few families of Jewish heritage.

The households consist of stay-at-home moms and dads who worked steady jobs with long hours and modest pay. The social environment of post war culture then, was so much different than today.

Neighborhoods were close knit, protective and friendly. If one family was experiencing hard times, every other family got involved to help.

Doors were mostly left unlocked. If there came a time when a mom had to run an errand outside the neighborhood, she knew her children would be looked after by everyone else. Meals and recipes were shared by everyone, every day, and food was never wasted, it was shared. It was all for one and one for all.

On a street such as ours it was normal to have as many as sixty row homes with just as many kids of all ages and backgrounds. Everyone played together and whatever toys and sports equipment they had, were communal and treated with respect.

Seldom was there an issue with kids from other neighborhoods walking through causing trouble. They respected our block and we respected theirs. However, on the off-chance a situation did arise, the entire clan would mobilize to quickly put it to rest.

The adventures in this book will give the reader some idea of what Bobby's life was like through his early years, elementary school, and high school.

It's a light hearted approach to growing up in what you might envision while watching an episode of *Happy Days* on TV.

It truly was a wonderful time in history. We didn't miss what we didn't have, there was no point of reference because no one we knew had a life any different than ours.

Our parents grew up during the depression era and those values were taught and passed along to their children. We learned to appreciate what we had and took care of those things. We knew if we didn't, they likely would not be able to be replaced.

So, sit back while you read on, put on an old episode of *Flash Gordon* or *Little Orphan Annie,* make yourself a hot cup of Ovaltine, if you can find it, grab your decoder ring, and immerse yourself in the adventures of Bobby and his friends.

CONTENT

WANTED POSTER
1954
ROBERT ALAN CIAMPITTI
AKA "BOBBY"

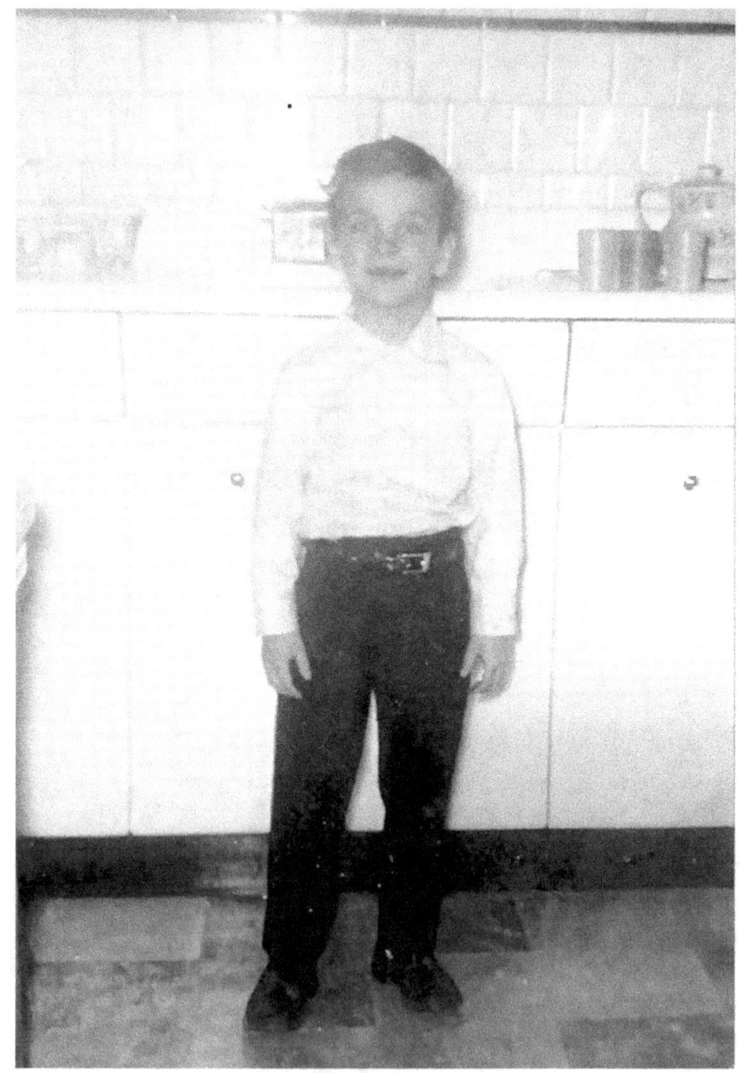

NOT ON A FBI POSTER, OR THE LOBBY OF A POST OFFICE!
BUT MY MOM'S KITCHEN ON DARIEN STREET

CHAPTER 1
I am Bobby

It's 8 am on a cool Saturday morning in September, school had just recently started, and I had just begun first grade at the Fells School located just a few blocks from where I lived. It was an easy walk back and forth from home and the neighborhood kids always walked together. We were either always early or always late, but together.

I am sitting at the kitchen table eating a bowl of Sugar Pops and a glass of chocolate milk. My mom is running between the kitchen and ironing in the living room, my brother Bill is sitting in front of the TV watching the latest episode of *Flash Gordon*. He loves that show; I hate science fiction crap but it's his thing and every kid has something.

There is a knock on the front door and my mom steps over my brother to see who is there, God forbid Billy gets up and misses Flash Gordon's papier-mâché spaceship landing on a poor excuse for a faraway planet that looks like Swiss cheese.

As my mom gets to the door there is a second knock, my mom yells, "Wait a minute," and opens it. Standing there in a light brown jacket, faded jeans, and an aviator hat with ear flaps is my best friend, Alfred.

"Is Bobby home?" Alfred asks.

My mom, with her hands on her hips and a stern look on her face, answers, "Hello Alfred. It's 8 o'clock in the morning, where else would he be?"

I hop over Flash Gordon, grab my hat and coat, and with a kiss on my mom's cheek, I rush past her and out the door, with my arm around Alfred's shoulder I ask, "What's up Al?"

Now Alfred has an older brother and two older sisters. His dad is a steel worker and although even-tempered, he is stern. Whenever I am over his house, we head straight up to his room to avoid the discerning looks from his dad. Al's mom is a sweetheart of a woman, and she is like a second mother to me, always has a smile on her face and a warm greeting. But on Saturdays, all of his family are home at the same time and Al just has to get out of the house as early as possible.

With a frown on his face Al says, "You know what it's like at my house on Saturday, so I thought I would come and get you and we could plan something fun to do with the other guys."

I had a nickel in my pocket, and with a smirk on my face and a quickened pace, we ran to the corner grocery store. Joe is the owner and a pleasant man who speaks with a broken English accent and always says, "Buongiorno!" His store is where all the neighborhood moms shop, he keeps a running total of what they purchase and collects from them at the end of each week when the husbands get paid. But for us, it's always the same.

"Bobby, you wanna TastyKake today?" Joe asks.

"Yes please," and with that exchange, I hand over my only nickel and walk outside to split it with Al.

We take a seat on the side steps of Joe's store, next to the open wooden crates of salted dried cod, in Italian it's called "merluzzo bianco" or "baccala". It smells like fish, but we are eating chocolate cake, so we hardly notice. Just as we are swallowing our last bite, the bakery truck pulls up to deliver the long loafs of Italian bread which are still warm. The aroma fills the air as the driver, Tony, we know his name because he is always the same delivery guy at the same time every day, carries the boxes of bread into Joe's store. We notice the rear door to the truck is still open and we look at each other with a devilish grin and sneak over to quickly snatch a loaf.

As we are running away Tony yells out, "You damn kids are going to jail one day!"

Several of the other kids are outside now and looking for us.

"Hey guys, where were you two?"

"Over at Joe's," we tell them, "We have a fresh loaf of bread that Tony gave us,"

Al looks at me, shakes his head and says that we probably are going to jail one day.

"It's like holy communion," I say and tear off a piece. I always get the nose of the loaf, it has the most crust, then hand the loaf over to the others to share.

We are all standing at the opposite corner of our street from where Joe's store is, near the pool hall, but not too close. We always stay away from that place. If our parents caught us near there, we would all be in big trouble. The pool hall belongs to the local wise guys, and they are the element of society we were taught to avoid.

So, with Alfred, Harry, Joey, Jerry, Sammy, Nicky, Richie, Butchie, Frankey and myself, we decide to walk down past the Fells School and over to where they are building a new Catholic church and school to see how far along they are. We all know that most likely when it is finished our parents would enroll us in the new parish. Now Fells School is ok, but we are mostly Italian, and all Italian families are Roman Catholic, so it's pretty much guaranteed we are all going to be in the new school.

Off we go, still chewing on the last morsels of Italian bread. Along the way, there are several houses with gardens in front. We pick off twigs, small branches, flowers, and seedlings from nearby trees. If you split the seeds open, the inside is sticky so you could paste them on your nose and look like a rhinoceros. With all of us pulling, picking, and snaping, the trail behind looked like a herd of sheep went foraging through the neighborhood. The owners are shouting at us, so we pick up the pace and keep going. It seems like we are always being yelled at for something, but I guess it's expected because every weekend it's the same routine.

Wow, they are really moving along with this project, the area is fenced off, but you can see stonework, heavy equipment, and lots of building material all over the site.

"Hey guys, there is a pile of wood over there outside the fence. It's not guarded so it must be ok to take some."

Al looks over at me and says, "You know we really are going to jail one day."

"Ah, come on Al, God must have known we needed his help and left it here for us. Let's grab a few pieces of wood and head back home. We can ask Joe if he has any empty wood crates, then we can make scooters. That would be great fun."

"How do you make a scooter out of this stuff?" they ask.

"Well, I saw one once. You take a flat board and nail it to the short side of the wooden crate, take apart one of your metal skates, nail one half to the front of the board and the other to the back, use an old piece of broom stick to make the handles for the tops of the crates, then nail bottle tops all over the front for decoration."

"That sounds cool."

"All we need is to take a few free pieces of wood and head back."

We were excited about making scooters, but I hoped none of the neighbors here were going to rat us out for taking the wood. I knew it wasn't free, but it was there, and we needed it. Just to be safe, I told everyone that since the wood was being taken from the church property that it would only be right to make the sign of the cross as we lifted the pieces.

Looking like a line of carpenter ants, we head back toward home. We have to walk past the hedges, flowers, and trees we scrubbed on our way here, so we have to move fast. And over to Joe's store we go to pick up some crates.

God, I thought, *I hope Tony isn't still there. He might throw us all in his truck and bring us back to his ovens.*

Once we have all the pieces, we need to make the scooters, I'll knock on my Uncle Nick's door for the tools. He was a master mechanic and lived across the street. He was my favorite uncle and liked teaching me how to build things.

We were in luck at Joes'.

He had several crates he was putting out for pickup and told us we can have them, "Just don't leave the rest of the trash all over the sidewalk."

"I'll clean it all up when we are done, Joe."

He tips his cap as a sign of appreciation.

The crates are around the side of his store and leaning against the wall just like he said. The problem was, only three were orange crates, the other two were fish crates.

The guys look at me with a smirk, "Who gets the fish crates?"

I pause for a minute, "OK, let's make five scooters and we can swap every once in a while."

We grab what we can and walk over to my Uncle Nick's house to see if he can help us out with the tools. My uncle is standing outside when we get there, hose and broom in hand, cleaning up the front of his house.

"Hi Uncle, what's going on?"

My Uncle Nick is a mountain of a man and always wearing his brown work hat, even when he is not working. He is an imposing figure in the neighborhood.

He stops what he is doing and says, "I promised your aunt I would get this done today. She is a little annoyed as I have been putting this off for weeks."

"Well, if we give you a hand, could you help us make a few scooters with the stuff we have?"

Looking over at our pile of boxes and wood, and looking over his glasses, he turns to me and asks, "Where did you get all the wood, Bobby?" he says in a low voice, "You didn't swipe this from somewhere?"

"No," I reply quicky, "it was a gift from the new church."

"The church," he says. "I don't want to hear any more so don't tell me."

I laid out my plan for the scooters and he told us, "Ok, you guys help me clean up and then we can build scooters." He pauses for a minute and says, "What's that smell?"

"Fish boxes," I told him. "Joe gave them to us for nothing."

"Gee," he says, "I can't imagine why! Ok, let's get started."

With all of us helping out, we finished in no time.

Just then, my Aunt Mary comes to the door and quips to my uncle, "So you got the boys to do your work; that's not nice."

"No!" he tells her, "It wasn't my idea. As usual, your nephew made me a proposition in exchange for my help in making scooters."

"Scooters!" my aunt snaps. Looking straight at me, she says, "I guess you are planning on riding them up and down the neighborhood, making all kind of noise from morning to night."

I just shrug my shoulders and say, "Well, we need to keep doing something to stay out of trouble."

With a crooked smile, she says, "Somehow, I know you will find a way to get in trouble no matter what!"

My uncle chimes in and says, "Oh Mary, leave the kid alone. You know how Bobby is, he likes doing things nobody else is doing. He likes building things."

"I know," she quips, "and you like encouraging him. You two make a great pair."

My uncle turns to me with a wink, "Ok guys, let's get those scooters done."

With my uncle's help, we move along quickly. Some of the guys are getting skates, some are painting the boxes and collecting enough bottle tops to decorate. Others are nailing the handles to the crates for steering. My uncle and I do the cutting; he only lets me use the saw because he showed me how and is confident that I won't cut my fingers off.

After about two hours, my aunt comes to the door with a pitcher of Kool Aid. "Are you guys finished making a racket yet?"

"Almost,," I tell her.

"Make sure you clean up the sidewalk."

"Ok," but in my mind, I am thinking, *nag, nag, nag!* I know my uncle is thinking the same thing!

"Wow, these scooters look great."

My uncle wipes his brow. "Yep!" he says, "Good job guys. Let's clean up and then you can go test them out."

I am so excited and proud of myself for thinking of this. If there was such a thing as a scooter showroom, I think these would be in the front window. Everyone gets a good laugh at that.

We are ready for the test drive. The first five guys are off and they work great, one quick spin and the next five guys are off.

"Thanks Uncle Nick."

Putting his hand on my shoulder, he says, "No problem, Bobby. Glad I was part of your plan."

My Aunt Mary is back at the front door, "What is all that noise Nick?"

"It's the kids' scooters," he tells her. " I guess you can't help making noise with steel wheels on a concrete sidewalk."

"Well, if I get any calls from the neighbors, I am blaming it all on you!"

Shaking his head, he tells her, "Well, why would this Bobby adventure be any different from any of the others?"

He gives us a wave and we are off, five loud scooters flying down Darien Street.

"What the hell?" I hear my uncle say.

There are a bunch of cats chasing after them.

With a laugh, I hear him say, "It must be the fish crates."

I turn around to see him shaking his head and laughing.

As I fly by my house, I yell to my brother, "Bill, look, I am Flash Gordon on a scooter."

My cousin Josephine is just leaving our house and standing with my mom on the top step. Josephine is my Uncle Nick and Aunt Mary's daughter and much older than I. She always laughs at the things I do and thinks I am kind of cute, always in trouble but always funny and unpredictable. My mom, of course, doesn't always feel the same way.

As we all ride out of sight, I can hear the neighbors chatting about where all that noise is coming from.

My Aunt Mary is on her front step and in a loud voice, she says, "Ask Nick!"

That puts a smirk on my mom's face and a hearty chuckle from Cousin Josephine.

This is how the process begins. A piece of wood, a hammer, some nails and a pair of skates. It also helps to gather some bottle caps for decorating the box to make your scooter special. **The look of determination and smirk on your face knowing the noise that it makes going down the street will drive the neighbors crazy. But that's the fun of it!**

Now that it's finished, I can try it out and make sure all the pieces are nailed down tight. Don't want the scooter coming apart halfway down the street.

Every kid had their own idea of what they wanted their scooter to look like. Something unique to them alone. But the satisfaction of having built it on your own always gave you a sense of pride and put a smile on your face. But thanks to men like my Uncle Nick, who would always say, "You can do anything you put your mind to."

———

Once all the kids had their scooters, you felt like a motor-cycle gang who protected your own street. You can just imagine the noise of all these scooters with steel wheels on concrete made going down the street.

My mom always made sure breakfast was on the table when we got down to the kitchen, always on time and always good.

A stylish trio: my mom, Aunt Angie and my biggest fan, Cousin Josephine. She always got a kick out of my antics.

CHAPTER 2
Chill in the Air

I like this weather much better than summer, at least you can breathe and have some outdoor fun without coming home soaking wet. You can always put on more clothes to keep warm, but you can only take off so much without getting in trouble.

The classrooms at Fells School are crowded and the desks are made for two kids to share. My desk partner is a cute little black girl named Martha; she has a pretty smile and long braided pigtails with ribbons on the ends. She is super friendly and for some reason always has her hand in my lap. I am too young to think anything of it, but she always wiggles her fingers and gives me a big smile. If I knew any better, I would have a big smile as well. You know the saying, "if I only knew then what I know now." She follows me around at recess every day and sometimes corners me against the iron fence and kisses me, shrugs her shoulders, and runs away. So strange to me, is she really a teenager just dressed up like a little kid, and why am I so clueless?

Then I realized, I am only in second grade, and this is math class not biology class.

This went on for a few weeks before my parents got a call from the school that they needed to speak to them about a situation in class. My parents give me a third-degree interrogation about what I must have done in school.

I have no clue what I tell them, but they just purse their lips and say, "Well, we'll find out tomorrow and until then you are grounded."

Now I know I am not always doing what I should but this one is a total mystery. Maybe I can ask my brother Bill to see what he can find out with his decoder ring. Nah, that won't work, Little Orphan Annie is too busy selling Ovaltine on TV to give a crap about my problems.

The next day my dad takes off from work and with my mom goes to see the principal at Fells School. Now I never found out what happened or what was said but when they got home, I stood there with my eyes closed waiting for the hammer to drop on my head, but nothing happened. They said nothing; they just walked past me. My mom went into the kitchen and my dad gave her a kiss goodbye, patted me on the head, and left for work.

What the hell happened? I thought, *Did I wander through a black hole? Am I in an alternate universe? Did Flash Gordon beam me up to his papier-mâché spaceship and somehow got me out of trouble?* No, not a word.

Then, out of nowhere, my mom asked if I was hungry and if I wanted a sandwich.

"No thanks, Mom," I say quickly, but my instincts tell me to get out of the house as quickly as I can before out of nowhere the grim reaper appears with a sickle and cuts my head off. "See you at dinner time, Mom," and out the door I go.

By now, school is over, and all my friends are waiting outside my house to find out if I was coming out in one piece or in a body bag. Apparently, everyone in the neighborhood knew of the school meeting with my parents but no one said anything. Alfred was the first to walk up to me with my friends close behind.

"What happened? What did you do?"

"I have no idea and I am not asking any questions. Let's go play football before it gets dark and forget about this mystery."

My parents didn't mention anything at dinner, and everything seemed normal again. My brother asked me what was going on.

"Nothing," I tell him, "just eat your chocolate pudding and shut up."

He shrugs his shoulders and looks down to finish desert.

Time to get my homework done for tomorrow. Maybe I'll find out something in class then.

The next day we are all walking to school as usual, in the school yard kids are lining up waiting for the bell to ring. Single file, we head into our classrooms. When I get there, I stop in my tracks, look around, and everything seems a little different. Classmates are banging into one another not knowing where to sit, all the desks are re-arranged.

Our teacher shouts out, "Everyone, look for your name on the desks and sit where you are told."

There is a scramble with coats and books flying everywhere.

I hear my name called out, "Bobby, you are sitting here in the front now."

Martha is no longer my desk partner; in fact, she is in a different classroom altogether. My new partner is a kid named Stanley, red hair and freckles with round glasses. He looks like Froggy in an *Our Gang* comedy show. Good grief, is this my punishment? I never saw Martha again at recess. She was always on the other side of the school yard with new kids. *Oh well,* I thought, things change quickly in kiddom! Life is good and I didn't get into any more trouble at school, at least for now.

Finally, the closing bell rings, and we all hook up at the corner of the school to walk home together.

"So, guys Halloween is next week and mischief night too, what should we do?"

Alfred blurts out that Butchie told him he had an idea and wanted to go over it with us and to meet him in front of his house after school. Now Butchie lives right next door to me; we always have fun coming up with crazy ideas. He has very permissive parents, his mother dotes on him constantly and lets him do almost anything he wants. His dad is a tailor and clothing manufacturer with a shop right next to the Italian market where my grandparents live. He is not Italian; he is Polish but an integral part of the fabric of our neighborhood. He is a funny man with a pleasant personality. How they ended up on Darien Street, I'll never know. But here they are, Bill, Rita, Butchie and their golden cocker spaniel. They are friends with my parents and our personal tailor. He measures me for pants and jackets all the time. He always calls me "Bobby MaGillicuddy". I never knew why, but he laughed every time he said it. I just shrugged my shoulders and stood there while he measured, listening to him constantly telling me not to move.

We're all back in the neighborhood now, drop off our bookbags at home, and wait for Butchie out front. When he comes out, he looks like Aramis from *The Three Musketeers*. His dad is making him a costume for Halloween, and he is wearing part of it already. It's a pretty good guess what he will be for Halloween!

Anyway, we all gather around and listen to his plan. He wants to make a life size dummy with material from his dad's shop.

"We'll make it look really scary and on mischief night, we'll tie it to the front railings of some houses, ring the doorbell, and watch the neighbors freak out when they open the door."

We all laugh. That would be so funny, then we could tie two front doors together and ring both doorbells and watch as each one tries to open their door. Since both front doors open inward, it will be impossible for either one to open. They will have to go out through the back alley then come around front to untie the doors. We are going to get in so much trouble if we get caught, but it's mischief night, so they shouldn't get too mad.

"Yeah!" I tell them, "Let's think this through, it's mischief night alright, but it's not hoodlum night."

"Oh! Come on Bobby. We won't get caught."

"Are you crazy Butchie? Who do you think they are going to blame? Joe the grocery guy or Tony the delivery guy? No, they are going to come looking for me!"

"Ah! we won't let you take the blame alone if we get caught. We'll all own up to doing it together."

"Oh, sure," I say, "That's what the apostles told Judas and look how that turned out!"

"Ok," Butchie says, "How about we tie the bumpers of two cars together and when a driver tries to move his car, it won't go anywhere."

"Butchie, are you sniffing airplane glue? What do you think will happen when one car pulls the bumper off the other car?"

"Oh, I didn't think of that."

"Ok, let's go back to the dummy idea. When do you want to start making the dummy? Halloween is two days away."

"Tomorrow is Saturday; how about we all meet in the morning and head over to my dad's tailor shop around 10, then we can go to Pat's Steaks for lunch."

"That works for me, I'll tell my mom I am going to go visit my grandmother and aunt around the corner. Everybody agreed?"

With a nod of heads, everyone is onboard.

"Ok, see you guys tomorrow."

I stay awake all night thinking of excuses I could come up with after things go terribly wrong; you know, Murphy's law. Well in my world, as limited as it is, Bobby's law is somewhat different. I don't think things are going to go wrong, I know things are going to go wrong!

All my tossing and turning wakes up my brother.

"What's going on Bobby?" he asks.

"Well, Butchie, me and the guys have a plan for mischief night, and you know how off the wall Butchie can be."

"Oh, you're being crazy. Besides, you never worry about stupid stuff like this. You're usually the kid behind all the insanity. Go to sleep, the sun will be up soon."

Yeah, I think to myself, *Wouldn't want to miss a new episode of Flash Gordon.* So, I just roll over and close my eyes. I must have dozed off quickly, only to be startled by the sound of something banging against the bedroom window. Rubbing my eyes, I go over to see the lifesaver box Butchie and I rigged up on a clothesline with a pully to send each other notes from our bedroom windows. Opening the window, a cold blast of air rushes in. I grab the box quickly so I don't wake up my brother who is buried under his blanket. The note in the box reads, "Are you ready? I'll meet you out front after I finish my cereal."

Great, I thought, *Let's enjoy the meal now, they don't serve Sugar Pops in jail.*

Rushing down stairs, I see my mom is already in the kitchen.

"Why are you up so early?" she turns and asks, "What's your hurry?"

I can tell by the look on her face she is suspicious. With a studder I say, "Oh nothing really, I'm going with Butchie to his dad's shop to work on some Halloween ideas."

I can tell by her facial expression she is not buying this for one second, but she doesn't follow up with more questions and tells me to sit and have my cereal before I go anywhere. Maybe she thinks she'll find out the real deal on the news later today or walk over to the post office and see a WANTED poster of me on the wall. Either way, the wheels are in motion to execute our plan.

I finish eating and after tipping the bowl to drink down the remaining sugar flavored milk, I kiss my mom, grab my hat and coat, and I am out the door. *That's odd,* I thought, *Billy is not planted on the floor in front of the TV and Flash Gordon will be taking off in his rocket ship soon. I shake my head and think, God, what a stupid show, maybe one Saturday the rocket ship will crash into a strange planet and Flash Gordon will be devoured by Martians then Billy will have to settle for watching Sky King and Penny. Another stupid show!*

Out front, Butchie and the guys are waiting.

"Come on Bobby, let's go."

"We have to make this dummy before his dad shows up for work at the shop."

"Are you kidding? His dad wouldn't care if we used a real person and covered him in scrap cloth."

"Hey," snaps Butchie, "My dad is a great guy. He would let me use new cloth, not scraps."

We all get a good laugh at that. But he is right, his parents let him do just about anything.

It's still early when we get to the shop so not a lot of workers are there yet.

"Let's get moving guys, maybe we can ask one of the seamstresses to help us sew the arms and legs together while we make a scarry looking head."

After a few hours, our test dummy is just about finished.

Butchie's dad walks over to see what we are doing. Scratching his head he asks, "What's with the dummy?"

"Ah! that's just Alfred," I say.

"Screw you, Bobby," Alfred snaps, "that's not funny."

Butchie's dad smiles and says, "Yeah, it kind of is," and walks away.

"Sorry Al, I was just kidding, no hard feelings. I'll buy you a Coke at Pat's at lunch."

I put my arm over his shoulder, and we all walk over to Pat's Steaks. It's just down the street from the tailor shop.

Pat's Steaks is a great outdoor place, there is always a line of people ordering sandwiches and drinks standing under the canopy.

The smell of onions, peppers, and meat on the grill can be sensed from two block away. It never closes and its famous for its steaks, just as famous as Philly pretzels, and Italian water ice.

We take our spot in line and like well-seasoned customers, place our order with all the proper lingo necessary to get what we want, like shouting, "I'll have one wit and one wit out," you either want fried onions or you don't. There is a sign out front telling new customers how to order and what language to use. If you don't get it right the first time, the guy behind the grill tells you to move out, go read the sign, and get back in line. It's so funny to see the look of strangers to this odd process; looking dazed and confused, they go back to look for the sign. The line is always long, and it has to keep moving. South Philly is like a world of its own and I love living here.

My grandparents and Aunt Angie live just one block away, the guys and I walk over to say hello just like I told my mother I would do. Besides, my Aunt Angie is my favorite person in the whole world outside of my parents and she loves seeing me; she always makes me feel special.

With a knock on her door, she is quick to come out and greet us all, "What are you boys up to?"

"We were just at Pat's and wanted to stop by and say hello."

"Ahh, that's so nice of you." She pauses and says, "Wait a minute, I have something for you boys," then retreats back inside.

We all look at each other and wait to see what my aunt has for us.

"Wow! Thanks Aunt Angie."

She hands us a bag of figs she picked from the big fig tree in her back yard. "Enjoy them boys."

I give her a kiss goodbye and we head back to the tailor shop to pick up Elmer. Oh yeah, we named the dummy Elmer. I was going to suggest we call him Alfred, but I knew that would really piss off the real Alfred big time.

While we were gone, Butchie's dad had his worker add fake hair, eyes, nose, and mouth to the scary head.

"What do you guys think?" his dad asks.

"Good grief, this thing looks almost real. It's going to scare the crap out of someone when they open their front door in the dark."

Hmm! I wonder what I should wear my first night in jail? I have a bad feeling about what Butchie has in his head. I don't think he is going to just want to scare one or two people at their front door.

So, we wrap Elmer up in brown paper and carry him back to Darien Street. Butchie takes him inside and we agree to meet up in the alley way behind his house when it gets dark. We don't want anyone seeing us bring Elmer out the front door, that would ruin our plan.

It's dark now and we meet up in the alleyway for the coming out party of Elmer. We follow the alley leading from his back yard to the corner of our street. Butchie has a lot of clothes line he took from his dad's shop, and we pick our first victim's house. It's Mr. Quimby's. He is a football coach at the high school, so he is used to pranks, we hope! Elmer is tied to the railing, and we ring the doorbell and run to hide behind parked cars, waiting for Mr. Quimby to open his door.

It opens and we hear him yell, "Holy shit, what is this? Who did this?"

He punches Elmer in the head and slams his door shut. Well, I guess he is not so used to pranks.

We quickly untie Elmer and run off to pick another house. This time, we pick Crazy Joe's house. He lives at the end of the street, alone and weird. He stays to himself and seldom socializes with others. All the kids in the neighborhood think he is crazy. It's a perfect house to put Elmer; he looks crazy too.

Again, we ring the doorbell and run to hide. When the door opens there is no response, Joe just stands there, staring at Elmer, then turns and goes back inside, but doesn't close the door. We wait to see what the hell is happening. Joe returns with a baseball bat and beats the crap out of poor Elmer.

He looks out at the street blindly and shouts, "Now that's scary!"

The door closes and the inside lights go off. We don't move, just look at each other trying to decide what to do.

"Ah, that sucks," says Butchie. He walks up alone, unties Elmer and drags his cloth ass down the street toward his house.

Catching up to him, we all are kind of disappointed our plan didn't work the way we thought. Just then, we see headlights turn the corner and slowly come down our street.

"I have an idea," Butchie says, "Everybody go hide."

As the car approaches, Butchie grabs beaten up Elmer and squats between two parked cars. Then, to our shock, throws Elmer in front of the moving car. It hits the windshield and falls in front of the car's grill. With the sound of screeching brakes, we hear the car door open and a driver yelling profanities. He picks up Elmer and turns to look for the culprits.

"You," he yells at me, "Did you throw this?"

I am standing like a deer in the headlights for a second, then I turn and hightail it out of there. The driver throws Elmer to the curb, gets in his car, and drives away.

The guys are laughing their asses off as I find them back in the alley.

"That was so funny Bobby, you should have seen your face when the guy yelled at you."

"Swell, thanks guys. Just as I thought, I was the one left holding the bag."

"No," Alfred says, "You were left holding the dummy!"

Everybody has a good laugh, but we have to go back and get Elmer. We can't just leave him at the curb. When neighbors find him in the morning, they will know it was us, or me! We can kiss getting any candy tomorrow night goodbye. The neighbors will probably give us all poison apples!

Sun's up! It's Sunday morning and today is Halloween. Then it hit me, last night. What is the neighborhood going to be like? What will the gossip be? Are the neighbors talking about the dummy tied to the railings or the driver of the car yelling in the middle of the street? Is Crazy Joe even more crazy today than yesterday?

Only one way to find out. It's early and my house is quiet, I'll send Butchie a note in the life saver box from my bedroom window and ask if he heard anything. A quick pull on the clothesline and he should get the box right away. I'll wait to see if he answers. Within a few minutes, the box is back at my window. The message says "NO". Nothing. Ok, see you outside.

I am dressed in a matter of minutes and down at the kitchen table. Where's my mom? A quick spin around and I see she is at the front door talking to Butchie's mother.

Holy crap! We must surely be in for it now! I pour myself a bowl of Rice Krispies and slice in a banana. *What the hell,* I think, *it's probably my last meal in freedom anyway.* I put on a happy face and wait for my mom to come in and tell me what reform school I'll be attending.

She walks in and sits next to me with one hand on the table and the other resting on her chin. I give her a blank look while still chewing on a slice of banana.

My mom clears her throat and says, "Did you hear anything strange last night when you guys were out doing whatever? What were you guys doing by the way?"

I look straight at her. She is obviously waiting for an answer or excuse for something she knows but doesn't think I know.

"Well, it was mischief night, so we went around throwing toilet paper over some of the parked cars." Without pausing I add, "We cleaned it all up before we came home. Why?" I ask.

"Butchie's mom told me Mrs. Secura across the street thought she heard a car hit something or someone in front of her house and a guy yelling at someone. But when she went outside, the car was driving away. Do you know anything about that?"

"Nope," I answer quickly and shove another spoon full of cereal in my mouth.

Getting impatient waiting for me to swallow my food so she can ask another question, she simply grunts, gets up, and pours herself a cup of coffee. She turns and just stares at me thinking I'll break and confess to something. I tell myself it won't work; I've been here before so I know how to play this hand.

Eventually, my mom goes about her routine. Putting my bowl in the sink, I wash up to head outside and let the guys know what's going down in the neighborhood. It's important that we all tell the same story. There comes a knock at the door. My mom rushes ahead of me to answer.

When she opens it, there stands Alfred, "Is Bobby home?"

My mom doesn't even answer, walking back inside, she passes by me and says, "Stay out of trouble."

"Ok." Closing the door behind me, I step outside.

You can feel tension in the air. The moms are on high alert and taking sneak peaks out the windows of their living rooms, watching us.

"Just wave at them," I say, "like everything is normal."

"Ok, let's forget last night. What are we doing for Halloween?"

Now having a devious mind, I tell the guys I figure each house we knock on, the moms are going make a mental note of our costumes before they put candy in our bag, so the same kid doesn't show up more than once. I have an idea to get more candy than we would usually. The plan is, we hit every house on our block then meet up at the corner and start to mix up the costumes and face masks so they can't recognize anything that looks like they saw before.

We strike out on a second round of candy gathering. For the most part, our plan is working. After doing enough damage, we head back to Butchie's house to sort out and swap candy. Carefully, we discard the junk, only keeping the best. We dump out all the bags. Wow, gee whiz, there is a truck load of candy here. We eat as much as we sort. Tomorrow I am sure we will all test positive for diabetes, but for now we are the candy kings. Believe it or not, it turned out to be a pretty good weekend, especially since we didn't end up in jail after all!

My friend Butchie, showcasing the Halloween costume his dad made for him, complete with a real sword. We had a hard time guessing who he was, but one of the Three Musketeers was a safe bet!

1955 - My second-grade class picture At Fells School

1954 - **In front of Fells School with a few of my first grade class-mates. I am on the far right.**

Hanging with friend Harry, a cute girl who I don't remember, and my brother Bill, decked out in our Davie Crocket coonskin hats and trusty toy weapons

Chapter 3
War Games

It hasn't been that long since the end of World War II. Most of our dads were in active duty and stationed somewhere in Europe. My dad was no different, but he never talked about those days. I know he was in military intelligence as a stenographer for General Bradley somewhere in France. My dad spoke and wrote perfect Italian but to hear him tell stories, when the army found out he was fluent in that language, they told him they were going to move him into a secret command of interrogator and place him behind enemy lines in an enemy uniform to gather information from Italian soldiers under the command of Benito Mussolini. If caught, he would be treated as a spy and probably shot. So funny, all of a sudden, when asked by his superiors to translate information in Italian, he said he couldn't, he didn't speak Italian.

"How the hell did you get into this unit?" they asked.

"I don't know," he replied.

His original unit had already shipped out; he couldn't reconnect with them. He told them he did take shorthand and was capable of typing seventy words a minute. And that is how he ended up as a stenographer of the general.

But my dad hated everything about war. He was against unnecessary combat and did not like guns. But for kids, the war was glorified on TV shows and in every motion picture house across the country. So, when all the guys in the neighborhood wanted to play army there were plenty of military items that they could get out of their dad's old duffel bag.

Problem is, there were two groups of kids in the neighborhood. Kids like my brother Bill and his group of friends who were all older than my friends. Needless to say, they got all the cool stuff, and they always wanted to be the U.S. Army. What choice did that leave me and my guys? we could either be German or Japanese. Nobody's father had any Japanese souvenirs; they were all stationed in Europe not the Pacific. But there were a few German items we managed to scavenge out of our dad's stuff. My dad had a number of Nazi items. Being in military intelligence, he sent home lots of photos, arm bands, Nazi crosses, and a few daggers. He would never have agreed to let me wear any of them, but I wanted to look just a cool as my brother's army. If we had to be the enemy, we could at least look the part. It was cool for a while, but when the kids wearing U.S. Army stuff saw what we were wearing, they just froze in their tracks.

"What the hell?" my brother said. "What do you think you're doing?"

"Well, we are going to lose in the end anyway. Why can't we look cool doing it?"

"Because you wearing Nazi stuff and some of the neighbors are going to be pissed."

"Like who?" I asked.

"For starters, Mrs. Levin, Mrs. Bown, Mrs. Rosen, Nate at the Jewish Deli on the corner, and that's just a few."

"Well then can we join you guys and wear some of the U.S. stuff?"

"No, we got it first. So you guys will have to just wear regular play clothes." Then he just turns and walks away.

"What should we do Bobby? We don't want to play army just wearing jeans and a plaid shirt. We'll look stupid."

"Hold on guys, I have an idea. Butchie, can you get a white sheet and some black felt ribbon from your dad's shop?"

"Sure," he says.

"Ok great, I'll meet you there and we can walk over to my grandmother's house. I can ask her to do something for me that will really make us look cool playing army."

Over to Uncle Nick's I go. He has a few wooded broom poles in his basement and with any luck he will let me have one.

Pole in hand, over to the tailor shop I go. Butchie is already out front waiting.

"Hi Bobby, I got the stuff you asked for. What did your dad say?"

"Nothing," he laughs, "he wasn't here."

I laugh and shake my head, "What else is new?"

It's hard to walk past Pat's Steaks with the aroma of steak sandwiches in the air and not want to get one.

"Hey Butch, want to share one?"

"Hell yeah!"

The line isn't that bad, about ten people, so we order and get ours quickly.

While we are eating, Butchie asks, "What's your idea?"

"A flag," I tell him, "a great big flag."

Perplexed, he asks, "What kind of flag?"

"A Nazi flag," I say.

That draws the attention of several other men eating steaks nearby.

"What the hell are you kids up to?" comes a question out of nowhere.

"We are playing army and we wanted to have a flag to beat up on."

Grunting, he goes back to eating his sandwich.

Butchie leans in a little. "Are you crazy? We are going to piss off a lot of neighbors."

"No, we are going to use it as a bad thing, not a good thing."

"I don't know about this," Butchie quips. "But if the shit hits the fan, this is all your idea."

"I just want those guys to let us have some of the U.S. Army stuff. Maybe with this, they will."

My grandmother and Aunt Angie are all smiles when we show up. With a big hug, my aunt asks what we were doing there.

"Well, I need a favor."

My aunt would never say no, and my grandmother speaks limited English so whatever my aunt tells her we want, she will just do it without question.

I lay out the white cloth on the kitchen table and make a Swastika with the black felt ribbon in the middle of the cloth. My aunt and grandmother are looking at what I made, and don't say a word. My grandmother goes to get her sewing needle, but my aunt's smile is upside down and she wants to know why I want to make a Nazi flag.

"Well, all the guys are playing army and I wanted to have something to show that the U.S. won the war."

Butchie is staring at the ceiling, whistling a tune as if he has no idea what's really happening. My Uncle Tony and Frankie were both Marines, so my aunt knows what that flag represents.

"Does you dad know you are doing this?"

"Oh sure, I even have the Nazi arm bands he brought home from the war to use."

My aunt doesn't seem too sure about this, but let's my grandmother make the flag for us anyway. When it's done, it looks real. The guys are going to freak out! Butchie tells me he thinks we should roll it up on the way home, so we don't attract any attention. I know he's right, so we wrap it around the broom stick, kiss my aunt and grandmother goodbye, and we are off. Back to the war zone on Darien Street.

All the guys and my brother's friend are hanging around not doing much when we show up. Unrolling the flag, everyone's eyes pop open and their jaws drop.

"Where did you get that?"

Again, Butchie is just looking at the sky and whistling.

"Come on Butchie," I whisper, "You know what we did."

"Yeah," he says, "I just went along with what you said, but this was all your idea."

"I got Grandmom to make it for me. What!"

My brother says, "You got Grandmom to make a Nazi flag? Do you want her to go to jail?"

Holy crap, I wasn't thinking about that. My grandmother was an Italian immigrant, and the Italians were on the side of Hitler during the war.

"Ok, ok, I'll just use it one time and then leave it in the basement."

Shaking their heads in disbelief, the guys take sides, and we start to play war games. Hiding in the alley ways, behind cars, and wherever we think we can make-believe we are shooting from. I grab the flag and start running up and down the street like the Nazis are in retreat. Everything seemed to be going swell. Little did I know the neighborhood phones were ringing off the hook, and it seems all the calls were going to my house because my mom rushes to the front door and is scouring the street looking for me. I hear her calling out my name over and over, so I quickly run to my house,

"What's wrong, Mom?"

"Are you serious?" she shouts. "Get in here right now and bring that damn flag with you!"

When I look around, it seems everyone has scattered.

"What do you think you are doing?"

There I stand, holding a flag with a swastika on it and a Nazi arm band.

"Go to your room, wait till your father gets home. You are in big trouble little man!"

Good grief, what am I going to tell my dad? He hates this army business to begin with, but his son parading around like a Hitler youth? He is going to be so pissed. This will make the dummy incident look like a Laurel and Hardy movie. There is nothing for me to do, just lay in bed looking at the ceiling and wondering at which orphanage they will drop me off. After a few hours, my brother comes in to see how I am doing.

Sitting on the edge of the bed, he just shakes his head and says, "Why is everything you do over the top? Can't you just be a regular kid and do regular things?"

I think to myself, *Where did you get that from, an episode of Flash Gordon?* Then I thought, *Maybe I should cut my brother some slack. After all, I am the one always in trouble.*

We hear the front door open and my dad's voice.

Billy looks at me with a change in tone and says, "You're on your own, kid."

"Thanks a lot!"

The bedroom door opens, and my brother rushes out with a, "Hi Dad," and quickly heads downstairs.

My dad sits on my bed and asks, "Well, Field Marshal Rommel, how was your day?"

I sit up and in a humble tone say, "I am so sorry, Dad. I didn't mean to disappoint you. We were just playing army and I got stuck being the enemy."

"Hmm," comes a response, but I can tell he is trying to conceal a little smirk. "You know why everyone is so upset, don't you? War is a terrible thing and lots of people die, like friends and relatives of some of the people on our street. That flag and armband brings up a lot of bad feelings."

"I get it, Dad. But I didn't mean to do that."

"I know you didn't, but you are going to have to apologize to some people and promise never to display those things again."

"Ok, Dad."

He gives me a hug and says, "Let's go have some dinner."

"Is it prison food?" I ask.

We both give a little chuckle and head downstairs. After dinner, I ask to be excused. I want to go make my penance to the neighbors before the night ends. It's not good to have to go to bed with bad feelings, I never liked that, so I figure others felt the same way. I'll just put this whole thing to rest like it never happened and think of another way to have fun.

During dinner, my mom tells us that in today's mail there was a notice that the new Catholic school and church are having registration for the upcoming school year. I knew where this was going.

My dad says, "Well, what do you think Rita?" That's my mom. "What are the other parents doing?"

"Apparently, most are going to register and put their kids in Catholic school. If we do, the boys won't have to keep going to the Epiphany church for Bible study. Their First Holy Communion and Confirmation will be at Stella Maris, that's the new school, and it's closer."

"Sounds ok to me," Dad says, "Let's talk to some of the others and make a decision."

I have a smile on my face thinking, *Great, it's like a new adventure, lots of unknowns and things to learn. That will bring all kinds of opportunities for me to explore.* But then a lightbulb goes off in my head. I heard a lot of stories from other kids who are already in Catholic school about how strict the nuns and teachers are. Making a switch from easy-going classes at Fells school to stormtrooper Saint Joseph Nuns at Stella Maris might not be so easy.

It's August and my birthday's coming up, so I'll focus on that and think about school later. Maybe it won't be so bad. Deep inside,

I know I am kidding myself, but I am only eight years old and allowed to live in a delusional world of my own.

Tomorrow, I'll go across the street and get Joann to help me plan my birthday. She goes with me every year to the five and dime to buy the decorations for the party. It's my eighth birthday, and since it's summer, all the kids in the neighborhood will be here. There are lots of kids on our street, so the party will be both inside and out front. It's not just kids that show up; their parents also come over to help my mom. Some bring food and special treats; almost everything is homemade, including the cake, which will be huge! That's up to my mom; she makes the best cakes. My grandparents, aunts, and uncles will be there along with my cousins. I have a new baby brother, Bruce. He's only one year old but I'll give him a party hat anyway.

Joann is a great help, picking out streamers, hats, horns, balloons, and party favors to give to my guests. With some help from my mom, Joann and I start turning our basement and dining room into a party place. It turns out great and she loves helping. She is my dance partner at all parties and always dresses to impress.

With the preparations done, there is nothing left to do but get ready. I can't wait to collect all the gifts and money cards that will be coming my way. My mom straightens my bow tie and reminds me to be polite, always act surprised when handed a gift or card, and put a smile on my face. My mom knows I care more about getting money than toys or games.

I look up and say, "Mom, I swear if Joey gives me another Parcheesi game, I'm not going to let him in!"

My mom grabs me by the shoulders, straightens me out, and says, "Yes, you will, and you'll put a smile on your face and say 'thank you'!"

"Mom, that will be three years in a row he gives me Parcheesi. Does his family have stock in Parker Brothers? I hate that game. I still have two in my room I haven't opened from the last two birthdays."

The doorbell starts to ring, that means my party is underway. The first guest is, of course, Joann and her mom.

"Hi Jo, everything looks swell. Can't wait for everyone to see what we did."

The door to our vestibule stays open and guests just start walking in.

"Hi Bobby. Happy birthday. Hope you like the gift."

"I'm sure I will," giving the box a quick shake. I hand it to Joann. She keeps everything organized, but of course, any cards I get go in my pocket, Joann is ok with that, she doesn't want to be responsible for taking money anyway.

Next through the door is my friend Joey, wrapped gift in hand. *Let me guess,* I think, *it's probably Parcheesi.* My mom gives me a stern look. I know what her eyes are saying, accept the gift, say thanks, and let him join the rest of the kids inside.

After all the kids are here, we head down to the basement. My dad has a record player set up with an unlimited supply of 45" records to dance to. Outside there are folding tables, chairs, and a large tub with beer, wine, and soda. It's for the adults who showed up to help out.

The party is a big success. It's time for opening the gifts. Lots of oohs and aahs. The next box to open is Joey's, tearing the wrapping paper, I act totally surprised. Wow! Parcheesi, just what I wanted. He has a big smile on his face. I am looking for the nearest trash can to toss it in, but I don't. My mom would be really upset and that would ruin the rest of the party. I hand it to Joann. She is laughing; she knows what I am thinking.

My mom brings out the cake, covered with lit candles. Everyone is singing, "Happy birthday." I blow them out and make a wish; it doesn't work, the Parcheesi game is still here. I get the first big slice, and everyone claps and wishes me good luck. It's a good time and I feel special, at least for tonight. Now I am the middle child in the house and with that, everything is about to change. I am not the oldest son and not the baby. I am just Bobby, Billy's brother.

1956 - My eighth birthday party, everyone is having a great time. As always, I am dancing with Joann who is wearing her fancy dress for a party.

My mom makes us pose for a photo which brings a smile to my face and **that of my brother Bill. I don't remember who the girls are but obviously, my mom wanted to include them in the photo.**

My close friends and partners in crime.

Top left; Leonard, my brother Bill, and Larry. Bottom Left: Joey {Parcheesi), Harry, Butchie, and my best friend Alfred.

1956 -Eight years old and dressed as a mirror image of my brother. It made my mom happy but I always felt like I lacked my own identity, which was one of the reasons I always ventured into a scheme that set me apart from normal childhood activities at my age.

CHAPTER 4
Down the Religious Path

Summer is over and registration to attend the new Catholic school have been submitted and approved. The same is true for most of the guys in the neighborhood. Things are very different at this school. For starters, there is a mandatory dress code. White shirt with collar, blue neck tie, and blue trousers.

Discipline is paramount. At Fells school, the kids just hang out in the school yard waiting for the bell to ring, then in no particular order the doors open, and you just walk to your classroom. No way will that fly in Catholic school. There is a first bell. Everyone is in a panic and rushes to their classroom's assigned spot in the school yard. Lining up single file by name and height, waiting for the second bell. That is when a teacher or St. Joseph's nun comes out, arms folded and tucked into the sleeves of her habit, in total silence. Everyone knows what that means, stand still, in silence, eyes straight ahead. When the second bell rings, the school yard looks like the exercise yard of a federal penitentiary.

I don't know whether to laugh or cry. Be careful what you wish for, I think, it might just come true. I'll just follow along and wait to see what comes next. Each classroom consists of sixty or seventy kids, all arranged in their seats in alphabetical order. It's so funny but scary at the same time.

The first few weeks are a rude awakening. It's a hardcore adjustment period. But, like most of the kids, I adjust and fall into the required pattern of behavior. Just in case you are wondering, patent leather shoes do reflect up, I spend more time picking my pencil up off the floor than reading my catechism. Sister Amunda Marie soon catches on and moves my seat to the front row! I soon become her so-called "devil's advocate". She watches me nonstop. But that's a topic for another story. Soon comes an opportunity to step up from hell to purgatory. Father McLaughlin, the head of the parish, wants to form a boys' choir and says a try-out will be held after lunch break. Along with my friends, we snap up the opportunity to join.

Walking into the new church for try-outs, which is attached to the school, we head up to the choir loft and are introduced to the choir leader, Mrs. Hynamin. We get some basic instructions and are handed a book of hymns and musical scores for every religious occasion. We all make the cut, but what else would you expect from Italian boys from South Philly? We can all sing, it's in our blood. After one of the practice sessions, I was called to the side and told I was going to be the center of some of the hymns because I was able to reach the range of high soprano. This is so cool; I am getting special attention and able to side step the ire of Sister Amunda Marie. I can tell she hates it every time Father McLaughlin comes in to get me for a special occasion. I always look back and give her a smile. Nuns aren't supposed to smoke, but I can see steam coming out from under her snow-white bib every time I do! That reminds me of a joke I heard once, "Is it ok for a priest to kiss a nun? Sure, as long as he doesn't get in the habit."

We are now a well-groomed boys' choir; we get to perform at other churches and special events at the nearby military bases. Midnight masses are always packed with parishioners, usually only candle light and very quiet, except for the sounds of the choir.

It's now Christmas Eve, midnight mass, and lots of people crowding into the church. After finishing one of the tear-jerking hymns, I can see many of the woman are crying. Can't have that, I thought. Leaning against the choir rail, I begin to push one of the large hymnals toward the edge of the loft with my leg. Little by little, closer and closer to the unretrievable result of the book falling onto the pew below.

Alfred sees what is happening and with his hands folded in prayer and a disapproving look on his face, he is shaking his head, "No, no, don't!"

Too late, the book is on its way to the pews below. With a startling crash, the book falls open next to an elderly woman who screams out in shock. The entire ceremony stops, the priest looks out to see what is happening. Mrs. Hynamin is totally embarrassed but doesn't know what happened. The guys in the choir know exactly what happened and are looking at me, trying not to laugh. After a few minutes, things get back to normal and mass continues.

My dad is at mass as well and is waiting for me in front of the church when my brother Bill, Larry, Alfred, and I walk out. With some of the churchgoers are telling us how beautiful the mass was, especially with all the hymns and music.

My dad, however, has a strange look on his face and asks, "What happened up there, Bobby?"

I say, "Why you asking me? It must have been the ghost of Christmas Past."

"I think it was more like the work of Bobby present! You're lucky it's too late to buy coal."

The guys are just smiling. My dad doesn't say another word.

All I hear is, "Ok guys, get in the car."

It's Christmas Eve and I guess he just let it slide.

On the way home, it started to snow, how cool! A white Christmas, maybe God had a good laugh and is telling me everything will be ok. Merry Christmas Bobby! In religion class, we are taught we are all made in the image and likeness of God, so I figure maybe God has a warped sense of humor too.

At home, my mom is making preparations for the fantastic Christmas meal later today. I can see she struggles to hide some of the gifts yet to be wrapped. I grab a cookie off the tray, kiss my parents good night and head off to bed. No sugar plum fairy dancing in my head, just the prospects of all the cool stuff that will be under the tree in the morning.

I wake up before anyone so I quietly sneak downstairs to check out the gifts just in case I need to switch name tags with my brothers' gifts. I don't want any Flash Gordon stuff. Everything looks alright. I grab another cookie and go up to wake my brother. Billy.

"It's Christmas. Let's go check out the tree."

He is wiping his eyes and yawning.

"I didn't hear any reindeer on the roof, but I saw a spaceship flying away."

He throws his pillow at me and says, "Knock it off, it's a cool show."

"Whatever you say. Let's go down."

All the unwrapping wakes my parents and little brother. Within a few minutes, the entire family is sitting around the tree. I can smell coffee coming from the kitchen as my mom pours a cup for herself and my dad, both now watching the frenzy. Billy gets a big metal Zepplin and I get an erector set.

"I'll build you a hanger for that later on Billy, don't want Sky King to steal it. Ha ha."

I just can't stop ribbing him about his shows, but truth is, he is a pretty swell brother to have, always saying nice things about me. But then again, he has so much to work with.

Later in the day, the house is full of family. It's easy to feel the love and happiness being shared, along with good food, homemade desserts, and lots and lots of wine and toasts with anisette that my mom's mother makes in her basement. Even my brother and I are allowed to sip and toast. It's Christmas and we are Italian.

There is food on the table, wine in the glasses, desert on the trays, gifts under the tree, and snow on the ground. Life is good!

With the holidays over, life settles into a dull rhythm. School, homework, dinner, sleep, breakfast, repeat! Saturday is choir practice and mass on Sunday. Geez! Just shoot me, the only thing to look forward to are snow days. At least I can make some money when it snows. The guys and I knock on doors and shovel. I need to find other ways to make money. With money, I have more options. I am still just a kid and hate that, but that's life in the city.

I need to do something to break the monotony. There's a high mass coming up this Sunday and we have been practicing all week for it, the bishop is coming to make a presentation and all nuns and priests are on high alert. The mass is scheduled for noon and the choir boys have been given red tunics with white collars to wear. I am up front in the loft, up against the railing next to the organ.

The mass is well-attended and the church is packed. Special music has been selected for this mass and several songs require me to sing solo. At the finish of the second song, I have the attention of everyone below. For some reason, I feel the devil on my shoulder. The plug for the organ is on the floor and I can shift a little to get it between my feet. If I wiggle even a little, the plug will start to come out of the socket. My mind is racing and I think for sure I am buying a one-way ticket to hell if I do this, but the urge is getting stronger. Communion is over and the choir is kneeling, chewing on the remnants of the Host. Alfred and my brother are watching me, both mouthing, "Don't do it." I am in the middle of singing, the invisible urchin on my shoulder is saying, "Do it, do it Bobby. It will be so funny." Pop goes the plug, the organ starts to wane and Mrs. Hynamin, now in a panic, continues to finger the keyboard, but nothing resembling music is coming from the organ.

Snaping back to my senses, I maneuver my feet and manage to get the plug back in the socket. The organ begins to come back to life but it sounds like the opening of a horror movie. Finally, Mrs. Hynamin regains her composure and just keeps playing. She looks over at me with an expression of gratitude.

I nod back and kneel down next to Alfred, who is kicking me under the pew and whispers, "You're not going to jail, you're going to hell," and starts laughing.

After mass is over, we are walking back home and laughing so hard we have to hold our crotches to stop from peeing ourselves. Even my brother is hysterical, that's a switch from his usual condescending comments. But I know he is just trying to keep me from getting in more trouble every time I leave the house.

Holy week is upon us now and religious events are pretty much every day through the season of Lent. Just in case you are not Catholic, Lent lasts for forty days leading up to Good Friday and Easter Sunday. There are masses day and night. It is required that each classroom of kids attend the masses either during the day or at night. We know how to get into the choir loft even if there is no music scheduled. The night masses and vigils are in a darkened church. From the loft, you can see all the adults and our classmates below.

"Hey Alfred, let's bring a few straws tomorrow night and we can shoot spitballs at some the kids we don't like so much, especially the girls."

"Is this another one of your 'I'm going to hell' stunts?"

"No, Lent is for penance, so we are just helping them repent."

Alfred looks at me and says, "Are you the anti-Christ?"

"Come on Al, it will be really funny."

"Maybe for us," Al says, "but not for them. We probably won't be in the choir much longer."

"Well then, let's not get caught. It's dark in the church, we can sneak in and out and not be seen if we are careful."

"You're my best friend, Bobby, but I swear, I don't know how your mind works. You are fun to be around but sometimes you scare the crap out of me!"

With my arm around him, we walk off smiling.

We are back at church for the 7 PM mass. It's Holy Thursday and every pew is full, standing room only. We wiggle our way past the people in the back of the church, behind the confessionals, and up the stairs to the pitch-black choir loft.

Alfred is tugging on my jacket, "We shouldn't be up here Bobby!"

"We can't hit anybody with a spit ball from downstairs. Everyone will see us, and our butts will be toast. Don't worry, after we pick off a few kids, we can stop in the confessional on the way out, tell father what we did, get our penance, be forgiven, and go home with a clean soul!"

Alfred pulls me to a stop and says, "You know, there really is something rotten in you."

Looking back at him I say, "Yeah, I know. But I am just a kid!"

Up at the rail we can see the kids from our class, especially the Irish girls, Mary Margaret and Colleen, sisters, two favorites. God, I hate how they never get in trouble. It's always the Italian boys getting yelled at. And I am always one of them. Gee whiz Bobby, imagine that! We can pick them off easy.

"That's it then, ok?"" Al says. "Then let's get out of here before lightning cracks through the window and strikes us dead."

"It's just a prank, not murder, Al."

With that, we take aim. Perfect, they both get hit in the back of the head, Colleen turns and punches the kid behind her. Startled, he hits her back, Crap, Sister goes over and grabs the boy, pulls him out of the pew, and drags him to the back of the church. We hustle down to the bottom of the stairs.

One of the church ushers stops us and asks, "What are you kids doing?"

"We wanted to go to confession," I tell him.

Looking around, he says, "That one is open; you both can go in."

Hands folded in prayer, we quickly enter the confessional, kneel down, and wait for the priest to slid open the grill.

"Bless you, my son," the priest says, "Begin."

I can hear the reprimand by the nun outside the door.

"Holy crap," comes out of my mouth. Again, crap, did I just say that out loud?

The priest whispers, "What was that you said?"

Quickly, I start, "Bless me father for I have sinned..." I just keep making up sins until I hear quiet outside. I leave the confessional and hurry out the side door of the church where Alfred is waiting.

We start walking fast, let's get out of here before anybody sees us.

Along the way I ask, "Did you confess to shooting spit balls in church?"

"Hell no," Al says.

"Me neither, I just added that I lied to my list of sins!"

"That's what I did too."

"See Al, you and I are just the same."

Sinking his head down, "I didn't use to be," he says. "The devil is waiting for us."

"Cheer up Al, tomorrow is Good Friday."

"What's that supposed to mean?"

"I don't know. It sounded ok in my head."

"We better go to mass early tomorrow and maybe confession again before we take communion. I don't want the Host to burn my tongue."

"Funny Al," I say. "Let's go home and eat."

The new Catholic school and church - Stella Maris "Virgin Mary of The Sea"

Although this is a recent photo of the school and church. When I was there, iron gates and fencing were not necessary but times have changed and that brings necessary adjustments. The fifties were a much safer time!

1958 - This is a typical scene, my mom is always looking for me and standing at the front door searching for me to come and put on a coat. This is also what every Saturday morning looked like at eight o'clock in the morning when my best friend Alfred would be standing there asking "Is Bobby home?"

Standing with my dad, Brother Billy, and my little brother Bruce. We are wearing the typical aviator leather hats with fur ear flaps.

CHAPTER 5

Love of God, Family, and Money

I look around my world and what do I see, everything revolves around the ability to buy things, to get ahead, and gain respect. My take from what I see is, you better have the bucks to back up your trucks!

Self-motivation, ambition, and drive seem to be the key, or at least that's my take on life. Of course, it's only the life of a ten-year-old boy. But that is where I am standing right now so that is my only point of reference. "How do I get there?" that's the big question. I have some ideas. My dad is a businessman but I don't think my ideas are going to sit well with him. I need to think outside the box. My dad was a child during the great depression and was forced to do many odd jobs to help out his family. It was out of necessity, not for fun. I have heard him say many times how tough it was back then and thank God that his children would not have to do what he did to survive.

I, on the other hand, thought making money any way you could was a good thing. In my mind, there was no job beneath me, especially at ten years of age. How many choices could there be? Mine were obviously limited. I had to come up with ways nobody thought of yet. I guess I'll run them past Alfred and Butchie and get their take on it.

Right off the bat, Alfred is already shaking his head and Butchie is on board with just about anything.

"You know Bobby," says Alfred, "they still have the electric chair over at Moyamensing Prison. It's only a short walk. Do you want to start walking over now?"

Butchie just laughs.

"God Al, you haven't heard the whole plan yet."

"Oh! I am sorry," he quips. "Does your plan get better as it goes along?"

"It does in my mind, and I can make money, my own money, not just the twenty-five- cent allowance a week I get from my parents."

"Oh! That's different then. With the money you earn, you could hire a lawyer," Al says.

First up, each year around this time, our priest makes visits to all the homes within the parish. The deal is, he talks for a few minutes with each family, blesses the house and everyone there, then asks for a donation.

"Let's start our own church, a children's church. I can dress up like a priest, Bible in hand, rosary beads on my belt get some holy cards from the church store on Broad Street and buy a holy water bottle. I can fill it from the fountain at church and with your help, knock on doors, ask if we can bless their house with holy water, give them a holy card and ask for a small donation for the poor. Hello! Are you guys ok?"

They are just standing there with their mouths open.

"Let me get this straight," Al says. "You want us to help you make believe you're a child priest, bless their house, and get money for the poor?"

Yes, I won't say I am a priest. I am only ten, nobody would believe that anyway, but I can pretend I am an altar boy, doing church work. We can put half the money in the poor box at church and keep the rest. It's really holy water and we are giving them a real holy card."

Alfred is dumbstruck.

Butchie says, "It's brilliant. I'm in. How do we get started?"

"I have the clothes and stuff; we just need to go buy the cards and bottle at the church store, then just start knocking on doors. I think Saturday is the best time to start. The church is open, and it will be easy to get the holy water. We can even have a mock mass in my basement with all the kids from the neighborhood, I'll hand out white Neco Wafers, pass around a collection basket and make a little more money.

We set out to start our church and Saturday is a big success. Every house we went to let us bless it and gave us a little donation. Even the mass I held in my basement was a huge success. There were so many kids and adults some had to stand on the steps because there wasn't enough room on the floor. I ran out of white Necco Wafers, so I had to switch to chocolate. I hope Jesus doesn't mind.

This church thing started out as a scheme, but it is turning into something else. I really start to believe in what I am doing, wearing my priest outfit more often, after school and on weekends. My parents are a little un-nerved but feel it is a harmless diversion. I sprinkle holy water on just about everything. Even when I visited my grandparents and Aunt Angie, I look like a little holy roller. My aunt is not embarrassed in the least, she takes me with her everywhere she goes and seems proud of me. It's a little strange because as I walk past people I don't even know; they nod their head or tip their hats just as they would for a real priest. But it is beginning to wear thin, and the little donations are drying up. Ok, snap out of it Bobby! Time for a change. And with that, father Bobby gets put in the closet.

My Uncle Nick's next-door neighbor is a union representative, and everyone calls him Lefty, don't know why, he's right-handed.

Anyway, one day I am visiting my uncle and Lefty says, "Bobby I have a few boxes of canvas tool bags the bricklayers were giving out at a union function. You want them?"

"Sure! I'll take them."

"What for?" my uncle asks.

"Well," pausing for a minute, I say, "I can sell them as clothes pin bag to the women in the neighborhood."

"That's a great idea," says Lefty.

"Don't encourage him," my uncle chimes in. "Things with Bobby are never simple."

"How many do you have Lefty?"

"About fifty."

"Well, if I sell them for a quarter, I can make over ten dollars. Great, where are they? I'll take them now. Then I can start right away."

Lefty and my uncle just smile.

"This kid is going places," Lefty says.

"Yeah, he is," my uncle replies. "We just are not sure where."

It takes me about a week, but eventually all the bags are gone. Too bad, I know I could have sold more.

Running into some of the guys, they ask, "Where have you been after school? We were looking for you."

"I was selling clothes pin bags,"

They look at each other, confused.

I just say, "Never mind, what's been happening?"

"Nothing much, just studying for school exams. They start next week, remember?"

"Crap, no, I forgot, I better get my act together, if I don't do well my parents will ground me, that means no more money. See you later guys, I need to go study."

It's almost dinner time when I walk in the house. I have two thoughts on my mind. How do I begin studying for exams and where do I stash the two pockets full of quarters I earned from selling clothes pin bags? My pants are sliding down from the weight! But it's a good feeling.

My mom tells me to wash up, dinner will be on the table in a few minutes.

"Ok Mom, what are we having?"

"Meatloaf!"

Good grief. I like meatloaf when it's just meatloaf, but my mom tries to hide vegetables in it. I hate most vegetables and peas are the worst, but they are easy to pick out with a fork and hide in my napkin.

Dinner time is when the family catches up on what is going on in our lives and tonight, the conversation is about school exams starting next week. The attention to Billy is limited because he has been home studying.

My dad turns to me and asks, "What about you, Bobby? Are you getting ready?"

My mom clears her throat as if to say, "Go ahead, tell you father what you've been doing instead of getting ready for exams."

"Well Dad, right after dinner I will be in my room studying tonight and all weekend if I need to. I'll be ready."

My mom chimes in with, "You better, or you'll be going to summer school."

Now rolling my eyes, "I know, Mom."

Again, my mom looks at me with a fixed glance. "You better tell your friends not to knock up and ask, 'Is Bobby home?'"

Monday morning is here, I am getting ready for school and in a little bit of a panic. I studied all weekend. Didn't make a dime, but I did study. We will have four exams each day for the next three day. If you haven't prepared in advance, there isn't much time to catch up. Rushing down to have breakfast and take one last long look at my books, I think I am ready. I switch up to Rice Krispies, maybe Snap, Crackle, or Pop will bring me good luck.

We are all in our classrooms, the pledge of allegiance and morning prayer are over, and we are instructed to be seated, put all books away, take out two pencils, and fold our hands on top of our desks. My stormtrooper nun is walking up and down each aisle, dropping the blue book binder containing the first exam.

As the sound of booklets hitting each desk continues, there comes a warning, "Keep your hands folded, don't touch the booklets, and keep your eyes down."

Everything seems ready, the room is dead silent.

Now come the instructions, "Open your booklet. You have thirty minutes to finish, at which time you will put your pencils down, close your book, and fold your hands. When told to, you will in single file bring your booklet to my desk and go back to your seat. Now begin!" comes the command.

As the exam starts, the nun is walking up and down each aisle with a pointer in one hand and a wooden ruler in the other. God help any kid caught looking over the shoulder of the kid in front of them or attempting to cheat in any way. If you get caught, you will wish you were being burned at the stake. It's hard to concentrate on your answers when you hear footsteps coming up behind you. It's like the angel of death breathing down your neck. Thank God, the first exam is over without incident and the remainder of exam week follows the same way.

The school has off on Thursday and on Friday we are all back in class to get the results of the exams. It's only a half-day. All the kids are getting their report cards to take home and show to our parents. You can tell by the look on kids' faces what their report card showed. If a kid was walking fast, they did well, if they were walking slowly, they were just trying to prolong the inevitable. My stride, that of my brother, and of our friends are a quick one. Thank God, maybe now I can get back to making money and I have a lead on something that Lefty told me was coming.

All the guys are happy about the exams, and we decide to go to Nat's Deli for lunch. A grilled cheese sandwich and a soda is twenty-five cents. I like hearing Nat or his wife take our order with a Yiddish accent. Just for fun, we make believe we don't know what they are saying just to make them say it again. It's not as mean as you think, the Jewish kids do the same thing at Joe's Italian grocery store.

It's been a good day so far and I can't wait for Lefty to get home from work so I can find out what he has for me. When I see my uncle's truck pull up our street, it's my clue that Lefty is home too.

Rushing over to his house, I can see he has two boxes on his front step. I knock and he comes to the door and tells me the boxes are for me.

"Really?" I open one. I see hundreds of yellow pencils with a union label stamped on them. Looking up, my eyes must be saying, "What are these?"

"They were left over from a union election; you can have them if you want."

"Sure," and as I walk away, I am wondering, *How can I make money with these?* I'll have to give this some thought.

It's Saturday morning and as usual I am at the table having my Sugar Corn Pops. My mom is at the stove when the doorbell rings. She turns and looks at me with a strange look on her face. I stop chewing and shrug my shoulders.

As she walks to the door, I hear her say, "I am going to strangle him. It's like Groundhog Day."

I hear the door open and looking like Alfalfa, Alfred blurts out, "Is Bobby home?"

I am already on my way to the door to prevent my mom from killing Alfred. Tripping over the leader of the Flash Gordon fan club, I give my mom a quick kiss on the cheek and walk out.

"Is your mom mad at me?"

"Nah! She just hates answering the door."

"So, what's up today?" Alfred asks.

I tell him about the pencils I got from Lefty and want to go over to Goldy's Toy Store on Seven Street to look for something. As we are walking over, I explain what I am thinking.

"If I can find a pirate kit with a black eye patch, that's all I need."

He doesn't get it, I can tell.

"I can use the eyepatch, put some of the pencils in a coffee cup, and stand on a corner for donations."

I realize I am walking by myself; Alfred has stopped in his tracks behind me.

"Bobby," Alfred says, "this is the worst idea you have ever had. I don't want any part of this."

"Ok, fine, just come with me to Goldy's."

We find what I am looking for and head back home. I take out the patch and give the rest of the kit to Alfred. We part ways.

"I'll see you later, Bobby. I hope they allow visitors at the jail house."

I grab a coffee cup and a hand full of pencils and head out to see if this works. Moving from corner to corner, but away from my street, I am getting coin donations from many people. At the end of the day, I have about three dollars in change. *Not bad,* I think, but as I walk in the door, my mom grabs hold of me, my dad is sitting on the sofa, both yelling, "What the hell were you thinking? We got calls from neighbors telling us you were playing a blind kid and taking money for pencils."

"That's it," my dad says. "You are grounded until we decide what to do with you. These are our neighbor, they know you are not blind."

"Well, they gave me money anyway, so what's that about?"

"Get out of our sight, Bobby. We'll talk to you later."

As I head up to my room, I think, *Gee whiz, making money shouldn't have to be so hard.*

My brother is sitting on his bed, shaking his head.

"What Billy?" I say, "I didn't hurt anybody. I was just trying to make some money."

"What is it with you and having to always be making money?"

"It's all I have," I tell him. "It's more fun than playing in the street, football, or baseball."

We live in the city and except for going to the movies on Saturday there is nothing for kids to do. It's boring to keep doing the same thing all the time.

He lays back with his hands behind his head and says, "Can't you find things to do without driving Mom and Dad crazy. I heard them talking about military school, you need to really think about what you are doing or planning to do, even if you don't think it's bad. Because most of your innocent ideas turn out to be bad. Not to mention your friends get in trouble just for helping you pull off your stunts."

"Ok, I'll think twice from now on, but I still want to make money doing things, even if I have to do it alone. I think Alfred's dad is going to tie him to a steel beam and throw him in the river."

"Not funny," says Billy, but then he laughs and says, "Well, that would make Mom happy! No more, 'Is Bobby home?' I would hate to see you go, but I would then have the room to myself."

"Well, I love you too, but that's not going to happen. I am going to change my ways."

I'm not going to stop trying to make money, I'm just going to find ways that won't get me into so much trouble! Time to make a change, again! Besides, my dad asked Lefty to stop giving me things to sell.

He told him, "You might come home one day and find out Bobby sold your house."

I didn't hear it firsthand, but Uncle Nick let me know what was going on.

THE OLD NEIGHBORHOOD
THE WAY IT LOOKS TODAY - 2022

1960 - My Aunt Mary, my mom's older sister. Although she always lets my Uncle Nick help with my crazy projects, she tries to keep things from getting out of control. She didn't smile much but her heart was always with family.

AUG 1960

JAN 1963

1962 - My Uncle Nick visiting at Christmas. He walked over fifteen city blocks in a snow storm to help put toys together, he loves doing those type of jobs.

CHAPTER 6

How We Get to Be Who We Are!

It's early May 1958 and a wave of reality has begun to wash over me. Maybe because I am getting older or maybe in part because of becoming aware of all the flags being put up in commemoration of Memorial Day which is only a week away. The end of the war is not that far from memory. There is a unified sense of pride everywhere you look. Being an American is everything, especially to the children of immigrants only one generation removed. I stand with a sense of superiority and pride at being special in the eyes of every other country in the world when they play the national anthem at the beginning of ball games and events. I place my right hand firmly over my heart and a chill almost always comes over me. I think about how lucky I am that my dad was part of the reason the world is now at peace. I remember vividly watching the preparation for the parade which will take place on both Memorial Day and the 4th of July. There will be flags and banners everywhere. Men once again put on the uniform of their military days and stand at attention at the curb line as the bands and post war auxiliary groups march by. I have an army cap that my dad gave me from his war souvenirs. I wear it proudly!

At the parade, there are troops of boy scouts also marching in formation with flags and scout banners flying in the wind. It struck a chord in me that I had not felt before. I wanted to be part of that somehow. I needed to find a way to put these new feeling toward a worthwhile cause. Back home, I started to ask questions about how to become a boy scout. One of our neighbors, Mr. Quimby, told me there was a local troop that had their meetings in the basement of our new church on Wednesday evenings. I asked my dad if he would take me to see about joining the troop. He agreed and felt it would be a positive influence. I told him I would ask my friend Alfred if he wanted to go, we could all go together.

Alfred was excited at the prospect and asked his dad who also agreed to go with us on Wednesday night. It turned out the troop leader lived right around the corner from us. We met the leaders and some of the scouts in the troop, a few of which I knew from school. We brought all the paperwork home to review and finally sign up to join.

Alfred and I were really excited, they talked about camping trips, hikes, fishing trips, and the jamboree for all scouts happening in July at Valley Forge. For city kids, this sounded like another world, but one I wanted to be part of.

Like it was yesterday, I have a mental picture of the scout master working in his basement, making gold stars covered in glitter in preparation for the 4th of July parade. He lived in the corner row home and his basement windows were easy to look through. I would stand outside looking in, watching him hard at work, making displays for the troop to carry in the parade.

I remember the feeling of being the son of a soldier and how so many didn't come home to their loved ones, and how blessed I really was.

My mom and Alfred's mom took us to a department store in center city to buy our scout uniforms, the patches, and neckerchiefs. This was amazing to me, I can't wait for the parade, the jamboree and, in August, summer camp. One whole week in the woods with lots of other troops from the area. What wonders would we experience? What new skills would be acquired? We would even have the opportunity to earn merit badges. That's how you advance in rank and move up in the troop.

The parade day is now here. The scouts and troop gather at the church to organize and prepare. My parents are there along with all the other parents, helping as best they can. The start of the parade is only a few blocks away and we march over to get in line with the others. Alfred and I are among the younger scouts, so we are at the front of the troop, holding the corners of our troop banner. The level of excitement is hard to explain. I never felt like this before, and I was hooked for sure. I was determined to ride this out to the end of the scouting line and do everything necessary to become an Eagle Scout.

The level of belonging to something special went over the moon when we camped out at the jamboree. We learned cooking skills, how to set up a camp site, how to start a fire without matches, and so much more. As evening drew near, all the troops began to assemble at the main parade ground. The opening ceremony was spectacular. Then out of nowhere came a group of scouts dressed as Native Americans dancing and chanting in a circular formation around the logs and branches that would make up the bonfire when lit. The chanting stops and the group stands in a circle as one lights a torch, walks over to the wood pile, and sets the logs ablaze. They turn to face the hundreds of scouts assembled around the perimeter of the site. One by one they call out the names of the scouts who will be initiated into the Order of the Arrow. When all the selected scouts have stepped out from their troop, they are led away to an undisclosed location to begin their secret initiation.

The remaining ceremony now begins and there are a number of high-ranking scouts who step forward, telling stories and sharing experiences that one day will be what each scout remembers they were a part of. The ceremony lasts well into the late-night hours until finally the closing is at hand. There is even a special procedure to end the night and extinguish the reaming embers of the bonfire. The scouts hike away from the ceremony, back to their respective camp sites, and prepare to retire for the evening.

At six in the morning, the troops are awakened by the sound of Revelry. The camp sites need to be broken down after breakfast, which is the responsibility of each troop. Police their area and leave it as we found it. By ten o'clock everyone is to assemble at the parade for the official closing of the jamboree. The flag ceremony, the anthem, and the final lowering and folding of the flag and farewells to all the new friends we met during the weekend from all over the country. Some will keep in touch, and some will become part of a fond memory.

This was Alfred's and my first exposure to being away from home and having to depend on ourselves. It was a liberating feeling and I felt comfortable in my own skin. *I can do this,* I thought. These experiences will make me even more self-confident and self-reliant. That has to be a good thing. I only hope my parents can handle it as well. Guess I will find out soon enough when they pick me up back at the church.

When we get back to the troop meeting room at church, all the parents of the scouts are there waiting.

The scout master addresses them first, "Before the scouts can leave, they must help clean up the gear and make sure everything is put back where it belongs. This is a scout troop, not a babysitting service." He turns toward us and commands, "All right troops, let's get to work. Your families are waiting for you."

It doesn't take long, but it is an exercise in discipline. I am sure most fathers can relate to that, having been in the military not so long ago.

I am so tired, but all I can do is go on and on about everything that happened over the weekend. My parents and brothers are listening attentively. They are excited that I am excited. It all looks promising for my getting their permission to attend scout summer camp next month. It is for an entire week, but on Wednesday, parents are allowed to show up at camp for a reunion with their scout and see first-hand what they have been doing.

My parents hesitantly sign the permission slip, and I bring it to the troop meeting on Wednesday, Alfred's parents sign off also. We will be going together. The scout master hands out a list of equipment and clothing needed for the week at camp. The mom's look at each other with an expression of, "Where do we get all this gear and the summer uniform?"

Without missing a beat, the scout master continues, "Everything you will need can be purchased at I. Goldbergs on 2nd and Market Street."

I am sure the next question they are asking themselves, "What is all of this going to cost, in addition to the cost of going to camp?" I can see it on my mom's face.

I walk over to her, tug on her arm for attention and tell her, "Mom, it's cheaper than bail."

That gets a smile as we walk off toward home.

The plan is for Alfred, his mom, my mom and I to head over to I. Goldbergs next Saturday. Camp is not far off and with the new summer uniforms, all the same patches have to be sewn on for identification as a troop. It almost feels like we are in the military. I love the feeling and it's not just playing; it's for real.

It's Saturday morning and we are off to get what we need for camp. I am amazed at this store. In addition to all sorts of hunting, fishing, and camping equipment and an entire section set aside for scouting, there are hundreds of military surplus items for sale. My mind is spinning. I don't know what to look at first. My mom grabs my arm and reminds me why we are here.

"Come on Bobby," she says. "We have lots to do to get you kids ready for camp."

Along with the essential items on the list, there is an item highlighted in capital letters, *"Make sure you purchase a quality pair of hiking boots, or your son will have to deal with blisters for the entire week."* Fortunately, there is a salesman to help with the correct fitting for boots. I never had boots like this, so it's something special. I lace up and trek through the aisles of the store to make sure they feel correct. Alfred is right behind me, and we are both all smiles. We are all set and heading for home with bags full of cool stuff.

Camp is only two weeks off and it's all we can do getting ready for what merit badges we want to work on for credit. Neither Alfred nor I know how to swim and are a little apprehensive about what will happen when we go off to the pool. The swimming merit badge is mandatory for a scout; one way or another, we have to learn.

The day is finally here, and my dad is loading up the car with all my gear to head over to the church to meet up with the whole troop. There will be a caravan of cars heading out, so no one gets lost along the way. On arrival, there is troop registration where our troop campsite is assigned. Heading off to the parking lot closest to our site is a short drive into the woods. Everyone lines up to get camp instructions. First, we need to set up tents before we can bring in all our personal gear. It's two to a tent and Alfred and I are camp mates. They have what is called the buddy system. No one goes off alone, your assigned buddy is with you at all times.

Finally, it's time to say goodbye to parents. They are given written travel instructions along with information for visitation day next Wednesday. After hugs and kisses, camp life begins. Orientation is in fifteen minutes, and everyone is to assemble on the parade grounds. There is a guided tour throughout the entire camp. Lots of trails and signs let scouts know where merit badge councilors are located, as well as the mess hall, the latrines, and the pools. They are an imposing sight and fear sets in, knowing when it is our troop's turn, all the scouts will have to get swimming certified, or you can't take part in any water-related activities. It's a must, and I am determined to do it. Alfred is nervous about this as well, but since we are buddies, when I go in, so will he, no choice in the matter.

At dinner mess, the troops get their respective schedule for the week. Our troop is scheduled for swimming certification first thing in the morning. It doesn't make it any easier to digest my meal. In a way it's kind of a relief to get it over with right at the start. Then I can concentrate on everything else I want to do.

It's Monday morning and we all line up for the hike to the swimming pool. We'll get breakfast afterward; they don't want scouts in the pool right after eating. We are all lined up at the pool's edge getting instructions from the life guards on what will happen and let us know that they will be watching each pair of buddies as we jump in and if for some reason it is necessary to get us out, they have long poles to let us grab onto and guide us to the low end. Two by two, we enter the pool, or should I say are thrown into the pool. There are guides in the water showing us how to float first, then how to stroke and kick our legs to get movement and confidence.

When Alfred and I enter the water, we first sink to the bottom but quickly float to the top where our guide is waiting. First there is panic, but with a little help, we get the routine in motion. What the hell? I am swimming and so is Alfred. The guide lets go and tells us we have to make it to the far end of the pool on our own in order to get certified. Reaching the far end, we jump out and with a big smile of accomplishment are handed our chip to take to the councilor to get our certificate. Now we feel like we are on top of the world; we can do anything they throw at us.

After breakfast, all scouts can pair off and go anywhere in the camp we want to as long as we are back for rollcall at lunch. Alfred and I are off to the rifle range to learn how to use a .22-caliber rifle on targets set up down range. This is a serious set up, the instructors are military-like and very strict and they should be; someone can get hurt if they don't follow the rules.

Camp is an amazing place for learning. Why every kid doesn't join scouts is surprising to me. Not even my brother Bill had any interest in scouting. But I have found a place where I feel I belong. There was one drawback. With everything I learned this year, I didn't learn to stay on the established paths. Walking through the weeds as a shortcut proved to be hazardous, poison ivy! As an inner-city kid, you don't come in contact with it, so I wasn't on the lookout for the three-leaf danger. In a matter of just one night, I woke up to itchy bumps everywhere. I went to our scout master who immediately told me what it was and sent both Alfred and me to the infirmary. Al wasn't as bad as I was, but still was in discomfort. The nurse gave us bottles of calamine lotion and told us to stay out of the sun and don't scratch. I went through the entire bottle in a few minutes and asked for another to take back to camp. She gave me two and told me I would need it.

Tomorrow was Wednesday, visitation day for parents. I looked forward to seeing them and telling them all about camp, what I have learned, and the merit badges I earned so far.

Cars start arriving at 8 AM and the camp is overrun with parents looking for their scouts. My parents are no different. Except they were met by our scout master and Alfred, who told them not to worry, I was at the infirmary with poison ivy, but they could follow the signs to see me or wait at the mess hall. My parents were already walking to the infirmary before he finished what he was saying. Alfred is walking along with them. He tells them he is my buddy, and he has to be wherever I am. He has poison ivy too but not so bad. They were not prepared for what they saw when they walked into the infirmary.

Hi Mom. Hi Dad," I said with smile on my face.

They just stood there with their mouths open, "What happened Bobby?"

The nurse explains what was going on and that I must be allergic to the poison more so than most kids. It was pretty bad and covered most of my visible body parts. But I wasn't disheartened, I just took it in stride and wanted to show them around camp. It looked like they were being escorted by a pink monster.

When we finally got back to my tent, Alfred went to the mess hall for lunch. My lunch was delivered to my tent because of my condition.

The scout master said he would bring something back for them to eat in a few minutes.

They were asking him if they should take me home.

"You can if he wants to go home, but he hasn't stopped doing anything yet because of the poison ivy."

They asked if I wanted to go.

"No," I said, "I want to stay to the end of the week." I had been working on merit badges and wanted to finish.

With regret in their eyes, they agree, and the scout master told them I was a determined scout, and he enjoyed my being in the troop, then went off to get lunch.

By the end of the week, I had earned six merit badges, including swimming. I was so proud of myself. But the strain of the week had finally caught up with me and when I got home, my mom told me to get in the tub filled with warm water and lots of corn starch. She spoke to our doctor who told them that it would make me feel less itchy, but the poison ivy would have to run its course.

Still, all in all, I had a great time and loved being a boy scout. I think my parents earned a merit badge as well for just having to endure what I put them through.

Chapter 7
Time to Expand

Summer is here and I have more time to find ways to have fun, maybe step away from "street crime," as my mom calls it. Alfred will be relieved for sure!

It's Saturday morning around 8 o'clock, yep, same routine as always. I am trying not to choke on my cereal and finish before there comes that inevitable knock on the front door!

"Bye Mom."

"Where you going?" she asks.

"To meet Alfred. We are going for a bike ride to Jerry's Corner."

"How do you know he is outside?"

Before I can even answer, we hear *knock, knock.* My mom just looks at me blankly.

"That's how I know. Bye Mom."

As I open the front door, Al starts, "Is Bobby..." Then stops and says, "There you are. Ok, still want to bike over to Jerry's Corner?"

"Yep, let's get going, it's a long ride."

Jerry's Corner is in a huge building, kind of like a bazaar, but it's on the other side of the river so we need to bike over the bridge to get there. It's our first time but we will be fine. The place is packed with shoppers and there are little booths set up all the way around the building. One booth has used clothing, shoes, belts, ties, and jackets.

"Al, I yell, come look at this. Aren't our parents putting together bags of used clothes for the church bazaar?"

"Yeah, my mom has lots of stuff she is sending over to the church."

"My mom does too. Why don't we take some of the stuff and make our own booth near the pool hall and sell it all to make some money?"

Al's eyes get big, as if a light bulb just went off in his head. "Great idea, let's head back and go through the bags."

Back at our houses, we are rummaging through the old clothes, picking out the best stuff to sell. Together, we have plenty of things, just like the booth at Jerry's Corner. As we start to set up our display, we realize we don't have any neckties. They would be a big seller. The pool hall is all guys, so that would have some appeal.

"Wait here Al, I am going to go back and see if I can find some in my dad's closet."

My dad is at work so I can't ask him for some ties, but there is a box on the floor with bowties, lots and lots of bowties. I figure they must be going in the church pile, so it should be fine if I take them for our stand.

Rushing back to the pool hall, I see Alfred talking to some older guys.

I butt in with, "I have some great bowties to look at."

"Where did you get those?" Al asks.

"From my dad. There are about twenty?"

"How much?" asks the guy shopping at our stand.

"Fifty cents each."

"Ok, I'll take these four."

"This was a great idea," I say with a smile.

By day's end, we sold everything we had and made almost eleven dollars each, that's a lot of money for a kid.

We clean up our spot and shake hands, "Good job, Al. See you tomorrow."

"Sure," then he pauses and asks, "Maybe we can bike over the Ben Franklin Bridge and get a hamburger at White Castle on the Jersey side?"

"Swell Al, we have plenty of money for that."

We split up and head home.

I rush in the house to tell my mom what a great day I had and didn't even get in any trouble.

She smiles and says, "That's a switch, tell me all about it."

Sitting at the kitchen table, I tell her how we saw these booths set up at Jerry's Corner selling used clothes.

My mom stops me and adds, "So that's why you were going through the bags I set aside for the church."

"Yeah! You were giving them away anyhow."

"Ok, go on," she says.

Just then, my dad walks in with a smile and asks, "What going on?"

Looking up, my mom says, "Bobby was just telling me about his clothing store at the end of the street today."

With a perplexed look on his face, he asks, "What clothing store?"

My mom responds, "I'll explain later. Go on Bobby, finish."

I explain how it all started with a guy wanting to buy bowties.

"Really?" my dad says, "Where did you get the bowties?"

"In your closet, in the box you were giving to the church."

Startled he says, "No, I wasn't. I was just keeping them for special occasions."

With that, he hurries upstairs, my mom doesn't even move, she is too busy laughing and shaking her head.

From upstairs we hear, "You took all of them?"

My head sinks down on my chest, "No, I left the black one. I didn't think it would sell."

My mom put her hand on my shoulder and just keeps laughing.

I look up and ask, "Should I go to my room now?"

"No, go wash up; it's almost dinner. I'll talk to your dad later. It'll be ok."

I think secretly my mom hated those bowties anyhow.

I am not crying, but I'm not happy either. I just can't seem to make this money-making thing work out. I'll just have to try something else. Maybe shine shoes, how much trouble can I possibly get into doing that? It's just me, a box, some polish, a rag, and a brush. I'll figure it out tomorrow. Tonight, I'll just chill out and do nothing.

So much for doing nothing. My mom comes in the living room and says, "Alfred's mother called and asked if you could go over and watch TV with Alfred."

"Sure, I'll head over now."

Al's parents are going out food shopping. TV is boring, nothing exciting to watch. Let's make some prank phone calls for fun. After three or four times calling the same number, we are rolling around laughing. Just then, his parents get home with food packages so we head up to his room to read comic books.

We can hear Alfred's dad talking with a woman at the front door who is obviously angry about something. Al's dad yells up for us to get downstairs. Apparently, the number we were calling belonged to the neighbor two doors down and they recognized our voices. Al's dad is really pissed and tells me it's time for me to go home.

With that, he grabs Al by the collar and says, "You dirty, rotten, stinking kid, go to your room. I'll deal with you after Bobby leaves."

I quickly grab my jacket, say goodbye, and leave. I hope his dad doesn't call my house, I'm in enough trouble for one day. Maybe tomorrow I'll go to Joe's and buy garlic to wear around my neck to keep evil spirits away. At least if I go to military school, I'll have company. Unfortunately, when you screw up in military school, I think they just stand you up and shoot you!

I don't hear anything bad brewing, so I just tell my parents I am going to bed. Tomorrow, I need to get my shoe shine box together and try to make a few bucks.

I have my shine box together and ready to head out. At first, I thought maybe the pool hall at the end of the street, but on second thought, that would be a bad move. None of the kids are allowed to be anywhere near the pool hall because of the wise guys who own the place. I decided to go up to the other corner near the shoe maker shop. It's a perfect place. They shine shoes there too but it's Sunday and they are closed so I think I am safe there. It starts out slowly. Then all of a sudden I am getting customers who are coming home from church. I am tired now. I did about twenty shines and with tips made fifteen dollars. My tips were much more than what I made for the shine. I won't tell my dad, but several of the shines were for the guys on their way to the pool hall. It was a strange mix of clients, to say the least, church goers and gangsters! I hate to say it, but the gangsters gave me a lot more money! (But that's a story for another time.)

Tomorrow, I'll try out the bar around the corner called the Porter House, guess it's because it's on Porter Street. Not a lot of brain power went into picking that name. Oh well, I figure, no one cares, it's a place for neighborhood guys to drink and hangout. Also, a great place to find customers wanting a shoe shine. I don't go inside. In fact I stand, on the corner, it's close to the bar but not on their front sidewalk. I am not allowed near this place either but it's where the money is, and I am doing pretty well.

It's getting close to dinner time and smelling the food from the bar, I am getting hungry. I pack up my stuff and start walking home; it's only a few blocks. I pass by Alfred's house and decide to stop and see how he is doing, you know, being grounded and stuff.

His mom answers the door and, with a smirk, looks at me and says, "You boys should be ashamed of yourselves, torturing that poor woman last night."

"Yeah, we're really sorry about that. We didn't mean any harm."

"Well, Alfred is still grounded but his dad won't be home for a while, if you want to go up and see him. But don't be long, he's in enough trouble."

"Thanks, I just want to say hi."

In his room, he is just lying on the bed reading comic books. "Hi Bobby, did you get in trouble too?"

"Nah, your father didn't rat me out to my dad, so I am ok for now."

"What did you do today?" he asks.

"Shine shoes, I made six bucks and fifteen yesterday."

"Wow, how many shoes did you do? A shine is only ten cents. Guys from the pool hall and in front of the Porter House bar."

Al pops up and whispers, "We're not allowed in either of those places."

"Yeah, I know. I didn't go inside or even stand out front. I was just nearby."

"You better not get caught; you know how our parents feel about those places."

Al's mom yells up, "Time to go Bobby; his dad will be home soon."

"Ok, I'll be right down. See you later Al, maybe you'll be allowed out tomorrow."

Finally, I am home after a long day out making money, especially for a ten-year-old kid. I am starving and can smell chicken cutlets coming from the kitchen.

"I am home, Mom."

"Go wash up and sit down for dinner. Dad is working late so he won't be home until later."

My brother Bill is already sitting at the table with my little brother Bruce.

As my mom is putting supper on the table, she asks, "What did you do today?"

"I was shining shoes and made six bucks."

"How? Where did you make that much money shining shoes?"

"Around the corner near the Porter House. Don't worry, I stayed a block away."

"You know your dad doesn't like you shining shoes. He had to do that during the depression and said he never wanted his children to ever have to do that."

"Yeah, but Mom, I made six dollars!"

"Don't let your father know and make sure you are always home before he gets home from work or for sure he will make you quit."

"I'll remember Mom, thanks."

"Ok, let's say grace and eat our dinner. I'll save your dad's for later."

My mom is a great cook, but she is second generation Italian, so that is nothing new.

After dinner, I am reading the *Boy's Life* magazine that came in the mail today. I notice an ad selling Burpee seeds. You can order a supply and after you sell the packets, you send back the money and get to keep a few packets. You also get credits toward a gift you can pick from their catalogue.

"Hey Mom, come look at this and let me know what you think."

After reading the ad, she says, "It looks ok. You don't need to send any money in advance so it can't hurt to try. It also says you can send back any packets that don't sell. Check with your dad, but it looks ok to me."

Later on, my dad gives me the ok as well, so I fill out the form and I'll mail it out tomorrow.

For now, I am still shining shoes and making a little money. But it's not very exciting. I know in the summer months the church sets up what they call neighborhood block parties. They get a city permit to close off the street at night. They set up booths in front of some of the houses and get volunteers to man them. They have lots of games for kids and gambling booths for adults. The head of the church ushers, Mr. Quimby, lives on our street and maybe he can help me set up a smaller version of a block party.

Just my luck, Mr. Quimby is outside playing half ball with my cousin Josephine's boyfriend Ronny.

"Hi guys," I butt in.

"Hi Bobby, what's up?" as they stop playing for a minute.

"Well, I have an idea for the neighborhood, but I need your help."

Mr. Quimby asks, "What can we do for you?"

"I want to have a smaller version of the church block party to raise money for charity."

Ronny laughs, "What charity is that? The Bobby prison fund?"

"Ha, ha, no, I can get the neighbors to help out and it will be a fun time for the kids too."

"So, what do you need from me?" Mr. Quimby asks.

"Do you think the church would let us use some of their booths and games for a weekend?"

After a short pause, he says, "I can ask Father McLaughlin, but I think he would let us. I'll find out on Sunday after mass."

"Great, I'll start to organizing things."

When Sunday masses are over, I sprint over to see Mr. Quimby. He has a smile on his face, so I know he has good news.

"Father said we can borrow some of the things we need, but he is holding me accountable, so no crazy stuff Bobby. Deal?" he says holding out his hand.

"Deal," and we shake on it. "I would like to have it all in place for next Friday and Saturday nights."

"I think we can get that done," he says.

"OK, I'll go ask Lefty to get us a permit from the city to close off Darien Street from 6 PM to 10 PM."

"How old are you again?" asks Mr. Quimby.

"Ten, why?" I ask. "I'll be eleven in August."

"Strange," he says, "sometimes I forget who I am talking to."

I don't know what he means, so I shrug my shoulders, "See you later," and rush over to see Lefty, who is outside talking with my Uncle Nick.

"What's up Bobby?" they both ask.

I tell them what I am planning with Mr. Quimby to have a block party next weekend and I need a city permit to close off the street.

My uncle looks at Lefty and says, "See what you started?"

But my uncle is always on my side and takes lots of grief from my aunt because of it, so I know he is only kidding.

Lefty rubs his chin and says, "Ok, but I might need a favor from you sometime later. Are you ok with that?"

"Deal," I say and hold out my hand to shake on it.

I feel like a big shot, wheeling and dealing with adults who don't treat me like a little kid, even though I am just a little kid. But I don't think of myself that way either. I can't wait to grow up. But what do I know, I am only a kid! Then I shake myself out of that nonsense thinking, no time for that now. I have work to do. Next weekend isn't far off.

Truth is, I am doing all this just to set up a booth to sell Burpee seeds. There is a gift in their catalogue I really want, and you need lots of points to get it. It's a camping set, knife, and hatchet in leather pouches. I think I can sell enough packets to reach my goal at the block party.

It's Friday afternoon and Mr. Quimby already has the booths in place. I round up the guys to help and by late afternoon, everything is in place. The city dropped off the barricades to close off the street after 6 PM.

The time finally arrives, and the street is packed with people from all over, not just our neighborhood. There are homemade cakes and cookies, pizza, hoagies, and games of all kinds. And yes, my Burpee seed booth. At the end of the weekend, we all clean up the street, take the church supplies back, and sit on Mr. Quimby's steps to see how we did. We managed to make enough to give the church three hundred dollars and split fifty dollars with all the guys. More importantly, I sold enough seed packets to get the camping set I wanted and even had points left over to get something for my mom. It was a great time. I make sure to thank everyone for all the help, especially Mr. Quimby and Lefty. I am feeling my oats. Now I am looking forward to my upcoming birthday and another game of Parcheesi. Good grief!

Funny, but worth mentioning here, that was 1959 and it's now 2021. I still have that camping kit! Thanks Uncle Nick! I learned from you to take care of my stuff and the tools you gave me as a kid. I still have them too!

CHAPTER 8
Being on the List

Capitalism at work, I must now be on the mailing list of every company trying to reach people to sell chances and merchandise door to door. Maybe because I sold so many Burpee seed packets in a short period of time, I would be a good repeat sales agent. From Burpee, I am getting offers to earn more points per packet and have access to even bigger prizes. But it's fall now, and seeds are not as hot an item as they were during the summer.

One such offer is a game of chance to win a large American Girl doll. The brochure shows the doll all gussied up with either blonde or brown hair and available in a choice of stylish dresses. They will send me two cards, each with sixty punchout holes with numbers on them. A player picks what number they want and writes their name on the card next to the matching number. When all the spots are full, the seller, "ME", punches out the large tab at the top of the card and it will reveal the winning number. Then, send in the card with the money and, in return, receive two dolls, one for the winner and one for the seller. Now I think to myself, what the hell am I going to do with a doll? How do I make money doing this? A bulb goes off in my head.

If I remove the winning tab with a razor blade, I will know the winning number in advance and buy that number myself, using a straw name, of course. Then I would end up with both dolls. Good so far! If I use the second card to sell more chances, I can actually get a real winner and give them one of the dolls I got for selling out the first card. Then award that doll, keep the second doll, and make fifteen dollars on the second card. This is a great idea. I only have to convince the neighbors to buy another chance. But with the holidays coming up, an American Girl doll would make a great Christmas Gift. That will be my selling pitch.

When the cards finally arrive, I show them to my mom, who thinks it would be ok to go door to door in the surrounding neighborhood to sell chances. Her advice is to bring the brochure with me to show that the chances are on the up and up. Good idea mom, I forgot to mention my plan with the second card. That would have killed the whole plan and me as well. By now my parents' patience is running thin with all my money-making schemes.

The sales are brisk and within a week I managed to sell all the spots on the card. My Aunt Angie bought the first four herself, she said if other people feel like they aren't the first, it will help them feel confident. In my mind, I decided right there and then, I was going to give the extra doll to my aunt. She doesn't need it, but she can give it to my cousin Rita who lives next door to her. Maybe that will elevate me to purgatory rather than straight to hell.

With the money from the first card in hand, I head over to the drug store to get a money order and, along with the card, send it all back to American Doll. Now all I have to do is wait. In the meantime, I begin to make the rounds door to door to sell out the second card. I feel as though I am a seasoned salesmen at this point so I begin my march on the streets I didn't solicit the first time, mostly because I sold out so quickly. And just like the first go around, I sell out in a few days.

After about two weeks, my mom tells me I got a package from United Parcel while I was at school. Rushing to open it, I find the two dolls as promised. Now I can punch out the winner in the second card and award the doll. As luck would have it, the winner is Rickey Paladino, our neighbor from across the street. That's great, I feel. It gives me creditability in the neighborhood. She is so excited; she has a small daughter so it will be a great gift. Now I can call my Aunt Angie and tell her she won also. My mom, however, seems a little skeptical at how I have two winners with one card. It seems everything I do raises eyebrows! Can't really blame my mom though, I do some really stupid stuff.

One of my less questionable jobs is making deliveries for Joe's Grocery Store to houses in the area. It's easy work and the tips are worthwhile. I make the deliveries after school but before dinner, so the housewives get what they need before supper.

The trick is how to maximize the tips. I have a small bank of money I work with. It's my own money, so I can pay Joe up front and collect when I deliver keeping whatever the housewife gives me. I always round up to the nearest dime and make sure when I give change. There are always quarters, not dollars, that way my tip will never be less than a quarter, sometimes more but never less. Especially if they forgot to order something they need right now, and I have to go back and get it for them. When I go back, I make sure I look like I was rushing for them and put on my cutest smile. That always gets a second tip.

I make deliveries almost every day and can average about three dollars a day. I don't work for Joe's on the weekend, I can make more money shining shoes on Saturday than I can in tips for a week. My mom knows I shine shoes but not my dad, he would never let me. He had to do that during the depression and hated it. But my mom said as long as I stay out of trouble and am back before my dad gets home for dinner, she doesn't mind.

Of course, she didn't know I was shining shoes in the pool hall and the bar around the corner. That would have changed the entire scenario. Getting into the pool hall was a trick on its own. I would have to knock on the side door and wait for someone to open the peep hole to make sure it was me before they opened the door. This was a private club, and the patrons were all part of the same family, if you get what I am saying. It's all guys, and they are all well-dressed, so they always want a shoe shine. It fits their persona!

Aside from the shine which is only about a quarter, they always give me a buck or two. No other kid was allowed in the pool hall to shine shoes, it was just me. There was a side benefit. The guys would take the time to show me how to play pool. How to make bank shots, how to shoot a combo, and how to leave the table when you don't have a good shot. They would place bets for one or two quarters and teach me when to match a bet and when to back away. What they were really teaching me was how to read the table and how to read the shooter, so I don't get hustled. You definitely won't learn that in school.

Just because I learned how to shoot pool at the pool hall doesn't mean I was learning to drink just because I was shining shoes at a bar. Although it did cross my mind. These were wise guys, not necessarily smart guys, but they were smart enough not to give liquor to a minor.

Learning how to play pool worked out fine for me. My cousin Josephine's boyfriend Ronny just happened to be an instructor at the local boys' club teaching kids how to play pool. He would let me play whenever I wanted and would set up matches for me with other kids. He convinced my dad to buy a pool table for our basement that he heard was for sale. Then I could play any time and perfect my skill. That would serve me well later in life. Ronny would never let me or any other kid play pool for money. The boys' club would not be pleased if that happened. So, I played for the pleasure of winning and learning. Once in a while, Ronny would teach me trick shots.

I was able to show off a little when I went to the pool hall to shine shoes and the guys there would place wagers on my making a trick shot. Of course, since I was just a kid, the winner of the bet would flip me a buck or two. I won a few bucks every day on one thing or another.

Now that we had our own pool table in the basement, my dad and his friends would come over and play pool. Ronnie would give them tips on how to make a shot or play a set up. Not to sound mean, but neither my dad nor any of his friends played very well.

Ronny would laugh and say, "Let Bobby show you how to make that shot."

Only Ronny knew I was learning how to play at the pool hall on the corner. They all thought I was learning at the boys' club. My dad would be totally pissed if he knew where I was half the time I was out of the house. But I couldn't see any harm in earning my own money.

The funny thing is, I would get a weekly allowance of a dollar which was up from a quarter just a few years ago. I would do the chores for my mom whether I got paid for it or not. The upside of doing chores for my mom was the neighbors would ask if I would do some chores for them as well and they would pay me for the work. So, in a way, my mom was providing advertisement for me without even knowing. I was getting odd jobs, painting the iron hand rails in front of houses, using reflective silver paint to freshen up the home address at the street curb line, and painting the wooden rear yard fences of every row home. If it snowed, I would shovel sidewalks and clean off cars. Christmas time, I would run holiday lights around the outside of homes and take them down after the new year. All small jobs, but there were plenty of them and always something to do whenever I had free time. Word was around that if you needed something done, you could call Bobby and he would find a way to get it done. I was fortunate that if I needed advice on how to do something I hadn't done before, I would call on my Uncle Nick for the knowhow and tools if I needed something special.

I had a lot of friends who would help me out with bigger jobs and take orders for work when a neighbor would stop them and ask if they could help get a job done. It was good for them too because I would pay them for any leads they got and for their help when they worked with me on a job.

We had a good thing going for a bunch of kids. Learning the value of a dollar, hard work, responsibility, and attention to detail. Not to mention it prevented me from coming up with ideas that usually got me in some kind of trouble. I think my parents also felt a sigh of relief that they knew what I was doing. It's not as exciting as some of my previous stunts but it was honest work. Good grief, I am starting to sound like a responsible adult. So not me!

AUG '60

Summer 1960 - Cousin Ronny, now cousin Josephine's husband, joking with my mom. He was a youth counselor at the local boys' club. He taught me how to make trick pool shots and perfect my play. Later in life, I was able to turn those skills into making money playing pool. That wasn't his goal, but it worked for me.

CHAPTER 9

Somewhere New

As a kid, I am more consumed with my own little world, not really paying attention to anything that doesn't directly impact my life. I am about to discover something new was going on with my family of which I had no clue.

It's a Saturday morning and we are all on our way to the New Jersey shore. That in and of itself is nothing new. We usually have a week vacation in Wildwood, and I figured this was that week. I never really liked going to the shore because I hated the feeling of sand, and all my friends were back home on Darien Street. But it was our yearly trip, so I just sucked it up and made the best of the week.

Almost three hours in a hot car, air-conditioned cars were not normal at the time. So here I am with my head out the window, listening and bouncing to the rhythm of a constant bump in the road for eighty miles. *God*, I think to myself, *is it Labor Day yet?*

I am not really paying much attention as we approach the exit ramp to Wildwood, but the smell of low tide, fish and mold whiff through the car window awakening me to our pending arrival at the seashore.

When my dad finally stops the car, we are at the end of a road where the paved portion stopped, and a gravel road continues.

Looking around, I ask, "Where are we?"

My mom and dad have a great big smile on their faces as they exit the car with my brothers and me close behind. Strange, they are just standing in front of this little bungalow, just staring at this house. Billy and I look at each other totally confused.

"Is this where we are staying this week?" I ask.

"No," my dad says, "this is where we are staying every summer." Turning to look at us, he continues, "This is our new summer home."

Wow, rushing back to get our bags out of the car, we run to the front porch and into the new house. We are jumping around checking out every room. We are so excited and not sure what to do first.

After we settle in and unpack, we decide to explore the area outside. We are the last house on the street surrounded by weeds and dirt roads. All I can think about is what to do now. There are no people around and no kids. Billy goes in for lunch and I decide to bike ride up the road and see what's happening. Maybe I'll run into other kids.

One thing for sure, there are lots of bugs here, and they all bite! That sucks, but it's not bad all the time, just most of the time. I ride my bike up and down a few streets nearby but no kids around. The first night is quickly approaching and my mom is making pasta. As we get ready to sit for dinner, we hear a loud speaker and voice coming from an old army Jeep driving by, announcing to shut your windows. A truck is close behind and is spraying for mosquitoes. Looking outside after shutting the windows, we see a bank of fog slowly creeping down the street directly behind the truck spraying for bugs.

"Let's get inside," my dad says.

You can smell the kerosene, which is what they are spraying, and it is thick enough to choke you.

The house is about 100 degrees with all the windows and doors closed. My parents have never experienced anything like this before, so they are not sure how safe it is to breathe. Better to wait for the fog to clear before opening up the house again. Finally, we can eat dinner and let the sea breeze flow.

There is no TV, so not much to do before bedtime. Maybe tomorrow will bring a new adventure. Lying in bed, my brothers and I feel like we are in another world. There are no nighttime sounds of crickets, bugs, and birds on Darien Street. As soon as you turn on a lamp, the screens are covered in bugs and moths.

The morning brings new perspective, It's peaceful and quiet. There is the smell of salt and sea hanging in the air. Totally different from the smell of trash trucks and manure left in the street from the vendors peddling their wares by horse-drawn carts.

Pancakes and sausage for breakfast, that's something special. I can get used to this for sure.

"Hey Billy, do you want to go look for signs of life?"

"Not now, I have something I want to do here. Maybe I'll catch up to you later."

"Fine," I say. "Mom, can I go for a bike ride around the area?"

"Ok, just be careful."

Jumping on my bike, I am off, Is there life on this planet? I travel through several streets and along the railroad tracks behind our house along the bay. Finally, up ahead I see a kid on a bike. Quickening my pace and shouting hello, I get closer. He is just looking at the bay but hears my voice and waves. That's a good sign; he's not a mirage.

"Hi, my name is Bobby. We just moved in down the street."

"I am Vince, are you here year-round?"

"No, just during the summer, I live in South Philly. You?" I ask.

"We live here all year long; my family has a restaurant over in the Villas."

"What's the Villas?"

"It's off the island on the mainland."

"Want to be friends?" I ask.

"Sure," he replies, "not a lot of kids around here. Want to bike over to the fishing docks down the road?"

"Ok, but I better let my parents know. Ride over with me, Vinny."

To my surprise there is another car in front of our house, it's the Sama's, Nick, Vera, and my brother's friend Larry. I guess that is what Billy was waiting for. I run in to say hello with my new friend.

"Hey Mom, Dad, this is my new friend Vinny."

"Hello Vinny, nice to meet you."

"Is it ok? I wanted to bike ride with Vinny. He wants to show me the fishing docks down the road."

"Don't be long Bobby. We were planning on going to the beach this afternoon, you included."

"We won't be too long."

The docks are huge. The fishing boats are really big and lots of activity all along the wharf. Fishing nets drying out, crates of fish on ice being wheeled up and down the docks. Vinny knows his way around, so I just follow him. He even knows some of the boat crew. His dad buys fish for his restaurant here every day. Even though I would rather stay here, I have to head back to go to the beach with my family. I hate the beach. On our way back, Vinny shows me where he lives and it's only a few blocks from our place.

"See you later Vinny, maybe I can stop over when we get back if that's ok with your folks."

"They will be at the restaurant so just come over."

It's a fun day at the beach with family and riding the waves, body surfing is a blast, but it fills my bathing suit with sand, and I hate that feeling. It sucks; walking back home with a crotch full of sand isn't fun.

The house has an outside shower and I get to go first. Mostly because I am doing all the complaining. I get dressed as fast as I can and head over to Vinny's. It's my first time in his house and it's pretty big, but no one is home, except Vinny. His room looks like a display in a German museum, but pre-World War II. He is very eccentric, over the top, and effervescent. He has rock and roll music playing and dressed up in a costume that looks like a mixture of military royalty and James Brown. He has a Keiser helmet on, the kind with the spike on top. My mind and eyes can't even process what I am seeing.

"Do your parents know you have all this stuff in your room?"

"Yeah," he says, "they are ok with it as long as I don't take it outside."

"Why?" I wonder. "Nobody seems to be outside anyway!"

"My parents let me do lots of stuff, they are always at the restaurant, so I have a lot of free time."

Shaking my head and with a smirk on my face, I tell him, "I have a friend like you back home."

Just my luck, I found the seashore version of Butchie!

I really like this kid, and we hit it off right from the start. I see him every day and he always has someplace new for us to bike to. My parents are ok with it as long as I tell them when I am leaving, where we are going, and what time I will be back home. Vinny has lived here his entire life, so he knows places to travel and make an adventure out of the day's activity.

We are here for a few weeks and my dad travels back to the city on Mondays for work and here again for the weekend. My Uncle Nick and Aunt Mary are here to keep my mom company, and Billy's friend Larry is here for the week as well. Vinny and I are pretty much on our own until the weekend; Saturday and Sunday I spend with family. My dad likes to go crabbing in the back bay or take the family to the beach. What a production that is, so much stuff: blankets, towels, chairs, umbrella, a cooler for the food and drinks, lotions, beach toys, cover ups, and so on and so forth. I'll say it again, I hate going to the beach!

We never go out on a boat because my dad doesn't swim, and we don't either. But every once in a while, we go out with my uncle for a four-hour deep-sea fishing trip. It's kind of funny, my uncle can swim but gets seasick on the boat and my dad can't swim but doesn't.

Week two of our vacation brings new bike adventures and Vinny asks if I want to bike over to his family restaurant for lunch. It's in the Villas so it's a long bike ride. Vinny knows some shortcuts through back wooded areas on dirt roads. Being a city boy, this is all new to me but exciting.

It's a cool looking restaurant, a very old school looking but still cool. His dad is the main chef and sets us up with all kinds of seafood and drinks. We need the energy for the bike ride home. Along the way, we are side by side and chatting about what to do next.

"Want to build a fort, Vinny? There is a vacant lot next to our house, it would be hidden by all the trees."

"Cool," says Vinny, "let's go check it out."

When we get back, my brother and Larry are outside. We tell them our plan and ask if they want to help.

"Sure, what do we have to do?"

"Well, you and Larry clear out a spot between the trees with the weed cutter and see if Uncle Nick will give you a hammer and some nails we can use. Vinny and I will go look for stuff to build a fort."

We are all off in different directions with a mission in mind, to build a fort!

On our first trip back to the lot, the clearing is looking great. Vinny and I drop off four "For Sale" signs we got from lawns in front of vacant house. As they keep clearing, we keep making round trips with signs until we finally have enough to start building our fort.

After a few hours, it's looking pretty cool. It's big enough for all of us and we can stand inside without hitting our heads. Back to the house we go, snatching up beach chairs and a small folding table. Billy grabs a bottle of Coke and a few sandwiches that were left over from the beach.

This is great, a hidden fort in the weeds, a hideout where we can play. Maybe we will even find other kids to hang out. The only problems are the bugs and poison ivy, between the calamine and bug lotion we all look like commandos! The afternoon flies by and we are all pretty tired. It's almost dinner time so we call it a day, we'll meet back here tomorrow. Maybe we'll go to the boardwalk tonight to play some games and ride the amusements. That would be fun, so we rush back to the house to get cleaned up.

But as we come out from the bushes, we notice two police cars in front of our house. Holy crap! What's going on now! We rush over to where my dad is speaking to a policeman.

Looking at me, my dad says, "We were just talking about you guys."

I swallow hard, "Why?"

"Well, it seems there have been calls about missing sale signs from the front of houses in the area. You kids know anything about that?"

I can tell from the look on my dad's face he already knows the answer to that question. Billy and Larry aren't saying a word.

As usual, I am the likely suspect, so I just come out with it, "We thought they were trash and we wanted to build a fort, so we used them."

"Where are they now?" my dad asks.

"There in the weeds down the street."

One police car drives off and the remaining officer, leans over. "Show me, son," he says.

Billy and Larry go inside, leaving me to lead the death march into the weeds.

The officer, standing with his hands on his hips says, "Pretty impressive fort, but you know you are going to have to bring all these signs back to where you got them. I don't think you were intending on stealing them, you were just borrowing them for a fort. Isn't that what happened, son?"

He has a hint of a smile on his face so I know what the answer should be.

"Yes officer, we didn't mean any harm."

"Ok then, he says, if you give me your word that tomorrow you and your friends will start putting them back where they belong, I think we can close this entire matter."

As we walk back toward the house, my dad thanks the officer and apologies for his son.

I hear the officer say, "No problem, kids will be kids. But your son is pretty clever for a little guy."

My dad says, "You don't know the half of it!"

Not sure what that means, but it doesn't sound like I am going to the gallows!

The next morning, we are sitting at breakfast. It's kind of quiet and I am just looking into my bowl of cereal, not wanting to catch a glimpse from my dad. I know what we have to do, I just want to get it done as quickly as possible. There is a knock at our front door, I let out a deep breath, thinking, *What now?* My mom gets up to answer. Great, it's only Vinny.

I can hear him ask, "Is Bobby home?"

I just start laughing as my mom turns toward me and says, "Great, another Alfred," and walks away.

"Hi Vinny, we have work to do." Walking out with Billy and Larry, I tell him, "I'll explain on the way to the fort."

Good grief, I've only been here for four days, and I am already in trouble with the police. It's going to be a long day!

This year, however, my birthday will be at the seashore. Not as big a deal as it is back home but who knows, maybe I'll get a fishing rod. My mom and aunt are making something special for a party, a strawberry shortcake with candles. It's mostly family and Larry's parents drove down for the weekend. I see my pal Vinny walking up to our door and rush to let him in before he knocks and asks "Is Bobby home?" That might drive my mom over the proverbial edge.

"Hi Bobby, happy birthday."

Vinny knows everyone except Larry's parents, so I am quick to introduce him.

"Vinny is my seashore Alfred I blurt out."

Vinny doesn't get it, but everyone else does with a chuckle.

After a homemade meal, my mom passes out all the birthday finery, hats, streamers, and horns. While we all whopping it up, my mom enters from the kitchen with the cake, candles aglow, singing "Happy Birthday". I get to blow them out and make a wish, it's a secret or it won't come true. And I won't disclose it here either.

After everyone gets a big slice of strawberry shortcake, I get to open my gifts. It's a swell birthday. I save Vinny's gift for last because I wanted him to feel special. We'll be leaving for Philadelphia soon and I won't see him again until next summer. I want him to know he is my friend; I don't think he has many here. When he hands me a card, it's amazing, it feels like it weighs five pounds. *What could it be?* I wonder. I tear open the envelope and it's a card, four pages thick, each page has pockets for ten quarters, there are really kind words of friendship on each page. I can tell he is watching to see my expression.

Reaching over, I put my hand on his shoulder and tell him, "We are friends, Vinny and always will be."

I can tell that meant a lot. I'm ten, not heartless!

AUG 1960 - My dad standing in front of the new "surprise" summer cottage in Wildwood, NJ. He was so proud of being able to achieve his lifelong dream. He thought about this during all his army days. He told us it was possible because of the GI Bill.

AUG 1960 -Bobby, on a pogo stick in front of the cottage. We didn't have a bicycle, so we made the best of what we had; it was better than just walking. It wasn't Very exciting but it's what I had, so I would just hop along and smile.

AUG 1960 - My little brother Bruce at five years old. He is sitting in the area where I would build a fort made out of real estate signs I collected from around the area. That didn't work out too well, but it was cool while it lasted.

CHAPTER 10
The Saga Continues

Summer has come and gone, and my sixth-grade school adventure awaits! All the same kids from the year before are all in their assigned seats. In Catholic school, not much changes. This year we have a teacher and not a nun. Miss Mary is her name, and she seems just as miserable as the nuns. I think to myself, this is going to be a fun year! NOT!

The usual antics take place at the beginning of each year, whoopee cushion on the teachers' chair, false teeth in the desk drawer, plastic dog poop on the floor. I, however, have long since grown out of that stage. I want to get through this year off the radar screen, make some money, and set my eyes on Christmas vacation.

I still shine shoes but now I am inside the pool hall and the Porter House tap room doing it, I know all the regular guys, so the tips are much better than average, and the owners pay me to make extra stops, but that's another story.

I have lots of ideas to make money this year. I could paint street addresses on the curb, paint iron hand rails, and shovel snow. Whatever happens, I'll find a way!

But as school starts this year, there is something new added, a carnival, right in the school yard. During class, we can see through the windows the activity going on, setting up tents, rides and lots of booths for games of chance. I've been to other carnivals in the area which had, in addition to what they are doing at our school, the side shows. Painted ladies, freaks, the tattoo man, the two-headed woman, and so on, this is a Catholic school so that stuff would never fly in the parish.

We are still allowed in the school yard for recess but told to stay away from the workers and equipment under construction. There is a really cool-looking ticket booth sitting just outside the fenced area. Me and some of the kids are playing ticket taker in the booth when the bell rings and recess is over. Like rats in a maze, everyone runs to their assigned spot in the yard, waiting for the second bell to go back inside.

As I look back, I can see Joey still in the ticket booth, trying to get out, but the door won't open. I am walking with my hands folded, not knowing what to do. I can't get out of line and go help him; punishment would rain down on me like fire from heaven if I did.

Back in class, Ms. Mary is taking roll call and there is one desk empty. "Where is Joey?"

I should have just kept my mouth shut but instead I tell her he is in the school yard, stuck in the ticket booth.

She looks out the window, turns to me, and says in an agitated tone, "ROBERT, go get him."

When we get back to the classroom, she sends us both down to the principal's office.

"Why me?" I ask.

"Because you probably locked him in there."

"Screw that," I say.

Now Catholic school kids don't talk like that, everyone else just freezes in their seats. Ms. Mary picks up a set of keys and throws them at me, hitting me just above the eye. Now I am bleeding and panic sets in. I instinctively run out of the room, holding my eye and head to the school nurse.

After a little ice and a small bandage, the nurse tells me everything is fine. But it's not fine. When I get back to the classroom, all the kids are sitting in silence and Mr. Mary is gone. There is a nun sitting at her desk who tells me to sit down and be quiet. I have no idea what is happening, but things are not right! The final bell rings, I gather my books and head outside to meet up with my brother and friends.

All the kids are talking about what happened and Billy asks me, "What did you do?"

"What did I do?" I snap back. "I didn't do anything, my crazy teacher threw her keys at me and hit me in the eye."

All the way home I think about how I am going to tell my parents, who I am sure by now know something happened with me at school. Now most parents of kids in Catholic school who get hit by a nun or teacher would say, "Well, you must have done something to deserve it," and my mom is no different, but not this time! My mom is pissed and by no means a shrinking violet, I can hear her telling my dad she is going to school tomorrow to confront Ms. Mary.

In my mind I am thinking that maybe my mom will want to take my baseball bat and play Al Capone on Ms. Mary's head. But I know that's not going to happen, too bad.

The next day, I leave for school with my friends just like normal. My mom tells me she will go to visit school later, not to worry. When we get to class, no Ms. Mary. There is a substitute nun in her place. Not a word about what happened yesterday; the lessons go on like they normally would.

I never found out what happened when my mom got to school, but the substitute nun is now permanent, no sign of Ms. Mary. I think to myself, *good riddance to bad garbage.* I knew this year was going to be different, but as usual, somehow, someway, I am in the middle of the event. I still have a red spot in my eye where the keys hit; it never went away.

The rest of the year flies by without incident. Final exams are here and summer break is just around the corner. I can't wait to finish the school year and maybe go to the seashore a little more often than before. We have a summer home now, I guess we will be going more often than just our usual two-week vacation. I can't help but wonder what changes have occurred since we were last there in August. I guess Vinny is still around, so at least I will have a friend to hang with there. Billy has his friend Larry who comes down with his parents for a few days at a time. But for some reason, Alfred has never been to the shore with us. I think my parents are closer to Larry's folks than Alfred's. Things change as you get older. Alfred is still my best friend and always there with me except during some of the summer.

It's Memorial Day weekend and we are driving to the shore to get the house ready for summer. My Uncle Nick and Aunt Mary are going also; he always helps my dad out with things like this. My dad is a really smart man but not mechanically inclined. Once when we were making room for a bureau in our bedroom, my dad was cutting a hole in the wall and without realizing, he cut through the electric lines and shorted out the system. Fortunately, my Uncle Nick was able to fix it before night time or we would have been in the dark all weekend.

We are finally there and get started quickly getting the house opened up and aired out. Everything at the shore smells like salt air and fish, but that's what the seashore smells like all the time. My uncle made window shutters for the front over the winter and is busy installing them, he asks me to help, and I jump at the chance. I like working with tools and my uncle teaches me more and more each time I do.

My dad is under the house crawl space, looking for the water main to the house. I am not sure how long that will take because he can't remember where it is and it's pretty dark and smelly down there.

Then I hear him call out, "I found it," and we see his legs emerging from the trap door. The house is now ready for summer occupancy. My mom and Aunt Mary start preparing dinner and Billy and I continue unpacking for the weekend.

After dinner, I decide to walk over to Vinny's house and let him know I am here for the weekend and soon will be coming down on weekends until school is finished in June. Vinny is home with his sister and grandmother, but his parents are at the restaurant.

Vinny has a big smile on his face and welcomes me back, "Come on in, Bobby. I've been wondering when you would be back."

As we enter his room, not much has changed. It looks like a museum from the early 1900s. He has a lot of 45" records and likes practicing his dance moves. He is so funny and bounces around the room like silly putty. I missed him too; I have a lot of friends back home, but nobody quite like him.

We listen to music and catch up on the last school year. It's getting dark and I need to get back to the house. I tell him we are having a cook out tomorrow and invite him over if he is not busy.

"Sure, I'll be there. What time?"

"How about three o'clock?"

"Ok, see you tomorrow, Bobby."

Sunday brings opportunity to explore and see what has changed since last summer. There is a new Italian deli that just opened a few blocks away on the same street as ours but still on the dirt road. It's called Tony's Market and along with my dad, we walk down to check it out. As it turns out, Tony and his wife are from South Philly and my dad knows them from the neighborhood. They are also the aunt and uncle of Bobby Rydel, a well-known singer at the time. Tony is a butcher so we can at least get fresh meat whenever we are here. The only thing they don't have are TastyKakes, but Tony tells me he will bring some boxes from home when he comes back next weekend.

"That would be great, thanks. But now we have to leave and get ready for our cookout at the house."

Vinny is already there and waiting for me on the front porch. We can smell all the Italian food wafting from the kitchen window. Vinny and I are making plans for the summer which will start in about three weeks. Tomorrow, we go back to Philly, and I need to prepare for final exams at school.

The school year is finally over and I pass to the next grade. But at this moment I really don't care much; I want to enjoy the summer.

My parents can't leave for the shore house yet, they have things to do in Philly and my dad is busy getting his new real estate office set up. There is an option. My Aunt Angie agreed to take me to the shore house for a long weekend, just her and I. Like I said earlier, she is my favorite aunt and would do almost anything for me. And it would give my mom a break from what would most likely be hair-raising Bobby events during the week.

We set a day we could leave and my aunt was looking forward to it as much as I was. It will be an adventure; we have to take a Greyhound bus from center city Philadelphia to Wildwood. My aunt packs sandwiches and drink for the trip, the bus stops along the way so passengers can have a break and maybe grab a snack. But it's crap compared to what my aunt brought. The trip is about three and a half hours, and the bus terminal is located in the center of Wildwood, from there we take a local bus to Wildwood Crest where our house is located. It's a short walk from the bus stop to the house and we hurry to open all the windows and unpack.

After dinner, my aunt asks if I want to walk to the ice cream parlor for a banana split.

"Sure, that sounds great!"

Along the way, we have to walk past Sun Set Lake; that is the back bay near our house. The sun was just setting over the water and you could see the sails of the boat anchored off shore.

My aunt pauses for minute and with her arm around me says, "That reminds me of one of my favorite songs."

"What's that?" I ask.

She looks at me with a warm smile and says, "Red Sails on a Sun Set".

I never forgot that. I think of her every time I pass by that lake.

The week passes quickly, and it's been fun being here with my aunt. For the last two nights, we walked to the boardwalk, which is a pretty long walk, but it was better than waiting for the bus which ran every forty-five minutes. It gave us a chance to talk about all kinds of things. I found out my aunt was engaged to marry my dad's best friend but called it off when he insisted on moving away from the neighborhood. She said she didn't want to be separated from her family and her nephews. I came to believe we were the most important thing for her, and she treated us all like her children. Anyway, if not for that trip, it was time I would have never had an opportunity to share with my aunt.

I found out my dad was coming down on Thursday and bringing his dad with him to stay with me for the rest of the week. He would take my aunt home and come back to pick us both up on Sunday.

It will be sad to see my aunt go and a new experience with my grandfather in charge. I never really spent much with him as I did with my mom's side of the family. My grandfather owned a candy store and ice cream parlor. He made his own wine, as did many Italian immigrants at that time. Every time he would send me to the basement to fill up a bottle for the dinner table, he made me whistle all the way down and back up the steps. That's how he knew I wasn't sipping the wine. It sounds funny now, but kind of a pain at that time.

So, Thursday comes, and my dad shows up with his father, shows him everything he needs to know about the house, and where things are kept. About three in the afternoon, my aunt leaves with my dad. I thank her for a great time and look forward to the next time she visits our summer house.

All this time, my friend Vinny had been finishing up school. Now he comes around early each morning to plan a day of adventure.

My grandfather likes fishing and crabbing and wants to walk over to the lake to see about renting a boat. He wants me to go with him to arrange for fishing rods, bait, and crab traps. I am not really into sitting in a boat all day for a fish, but I don't have much of a choice.

So, there we are in a small motor boat. At least we don't have to row around the lake. My grandfather is sitting in front, giving me directions of where he wants me to steer the boat. For hours, we bounce around the lake without much luck. Finally, I have an idea to break the monotony. I'll run the bow directly into the high grass; that will stir up the bugs and drive my grandfather crazy. My hope is that he will tell me to bring the boat back to the dock and be done with this fishing trip. I know one day this might send me to hell, but it's worth the risk.

As my grandfather starts pointing in all different directions he wants me to steer the boat, I make believe I don't hear him. He doesn't turn around, he just points with his arms and as I get closer to the weeds, he grabs hold of his hat. The bow cruises head long into the high grass, and you can see bugs and birds flying everywhere. Finally, he turns to look at me and yells for me to back up and get out of the marsh. I can't stop laughing as he is shaking his fist and saying something in Italian that I don't understand, but I get the message.

"Ok Grandpop." The outboard motor was stuck. "It wouldn't turn," I tell him.

"Let's go back to the dock," he snaps,

"Ok Grandpop, I am going!" It was so funny, and I don't think he'll want to go fishing in the lake again anytime soon.

It's now dinner time and after a meal of pasta and meatballs, I am cleaning up and my grandfather goes to sit on the front porch with a glass of wine and a few puffs of his little cigar. I get to join him with a small glass that he fills with some of his homemade wine.

He clicks my glass, "Saluto Bobby!"

It was a good day! I feel a little bad, but it was fun.

It's getting dark and the bugs are out. My grandfather goes to bed pretty early and he decides to sleep on the lounge chair in the living room. Now, he might be from the old country, but he isn't stupid. He knows there might be a chance I would go out and meet up with my friend Vinny. I figure he feels if he stations himself between my bedroom and the front door, he would hear me if I tried.

What he didn't count on was my ability to climb out my bedroom window. I had prearranged with Vinny to meet me at the rear of my house at my bedroom window and he could help me get out without any noise. True to form, after I heard my grandfather snoring and knew he was sound asleep, I quietly opened my window. With a smile, I see Vinny standing there with a wooden box for me to step out on to. I managed to close the window without making too much noise, then peeking through the front window I am sure I didn't wake my grandfather.

Vinny and I head off into the night, not really sure where we were going or what we are looking to do. We knew we had to stay in Wildwood Crest, too many police in the center of town because that is where all the clubs, bars, and the boardwalk are located. We walk down to the beach to sit on the seawall, looking out at the breaking waves on the shore under the moonlight.

Vinny starts telling me about the hard time one of his classmates gave him all year long, but never getting in trouble because the kid's father was related to the principal of the school. The more he talks about it, the more pissed he gets. Looking at me, he asks if I would help him get even with the kid.

"Sure, what did you have in mind?"

Reaching into his backpack, he takes out four boxes of red Rit Dye.

"What are you going to do with those?" I ask.

"Well, his family owns a motel here in the crest. They just opened the pool but the motel isn't open yet so there won't be any people around when we get there."

"And?" I ask.

"We could sneak up and empty the dye into the pool. With the pool filters running all night, it won't take long to turn the entire pool bright red."

"What if we get caught? Vinny, you are a local, I'm not. The local police will remember me from the signs we took last year and that won't work out well for me."

"Ok, you can be the lookout and I'll sneak in and dump the boxes of dye."

On the way to the motel, we are working out in our mind exactly how this stunt will go. When we get there, the place is dark. Only a street light casts a glow on the pool area. Hiding in the weeds, Vinny tears open all four boxes of dye. As he crawls around to the pool gate, I focus on the street, making sure there are no headlights coming down from either direction. Knowing we are in the clear, we run off to get as far away from the motel as possible. Just then, we see a car coming down a side street. Crap, it's a police car, no light or siren, it must just be patrolling the area. I am not taking any chances, so I jump behind some bushes. Vinny stands in the middle of the lawn posing like a statue, the patrol car spotlight is just scanning the surroundings. As it approaches, the light swiftly passes over Vinny and just keeps going. Wow, that was close. I think we should call it a night and catch up in the morning.

Vinny says he can't wait to hear about the motel pool in the morning. But for now, he at least feels vindicated. Back at my house, he helps me in the rear window and goes off to his own house. If this is how the season starts, I can't imagine what the rest of the summer will bring. I know one thing for sure, I don't look good in stripes!

1957 - Fourth Grade Stella Maris School

In a classroom of seventy kids, learning was difficult, everyone was treated as being of the same learning level. It was difficult to keep up but if you didn't, there was no special attention given.

I am standing against the blackboard, second from the left. In the rear of the room, far left, stands the giraffe, our teacher, Miss Mary. She was what my mother would call a frustrated virgin, mean and ill-tempered. I hated her! At one point, because she thought I was talking, threw a set of keys at me and hit me just above my left eye. I still have a blood spot in that eye to this day. I hope somewhere along the line, she got the same treatment.

1957 - Fourth Grade Class Picture

Fourth grade was tough for me. Even though Catholic School has lots of rules, Miss Mary made it even more unpleasant and her class was like a prison ward. I, on the other hand, put a smile on my face, kept the dress code and always put a white pocket square in my jacket and wouldn't let anyone keep me from moving in the direction I chose for myself.

CHAPTER 11
The Summer That Made Local History

It's mid-June 1962 and elementary school is over. In September, I will be in high school. Although I will be attending a private Quaker School instead of going with my friends to Bishop Neumann. For now, I am putting that out of my mind and focusing on summer.

This year I am working as a carpenter's apprentice with a builder my dad knows at the shore. That means I will be at the summer house for most of the season. Vinny is still just as unique as ever but now he is much more outgoing and has several new friends from Philadelphia who have summer homes in Wildwood. Now it's like a gang of kids all looking for a memorable season.

It's easy for all of us to get together now as we have new-found freedom from adult supervision. Most of our evenings are spend at the boardwalk, starlight ballroom, or the local pool hall. One of the new kids is the grandson of a well know cheese maker located in the Italian market back home and I know him and his family. They have an Italian grocery store in the center of Wildwood which is great. His name is Mario and every time we get together, he brings some food from his father's store. It's always good stuff, but it's Italian so you would expect nothing less.

Mario is a funny kid and likes to play pranks on unsuspecting people. One night we are hanging out near the boardwalk only a few blocks from Mario's family store. He is carrying a large shopping bag with six egg cartons inside.

"Hey Mario, are you getting ready for breakfast?" in a joking manner.

"No," he says, and starts laughing at what he has in mind.

We are all clueless.

So, he continues, "You know where the big roller coaster is on Schellenger Ave?"

"Yeah, we know."

"Well did you ever notice that the roller coaster cars are at street level just before it starts its incline to the top."

Again, "Yeah!"

"The only thing that separates the chain of the cars from the sidewalk is a six-foot-high fence."

All of a sudden, a picture begins to materialize in my mind as Mario continues.

"We stand at the fence with the cartons of eggs and wait for the cars to come by, then just toss the eggs over the fence onto all the people in the cars. They will have to go through the entire ride covered in eggs before they can do anything about the mess."

"So," I tell him, "the yokes on them!"

We all get a good laugh at that and with eggs in hand, walk over to the fence.

As the first line of cars comes down the track, you can see the look of surprise on the faces of the riders as the barrage of eggs begin to fly over the fence. It's hysterical watching from behind as the cars are heading up the track to the top. The ride is so fast, the egg droppings will have dried in place by the end of the ride.

Up on the boardwalk, where the ride begins, you can see a look of bewilderment on the ticket takers' faces as they try to help those getting off the ride to clean up. When we see a police scooter heading over to the ride, we know it's time to leave before anyone recognizes us. It's a riot, but no one was hurt. It was just mischief. Of course, that's easy for us to say, we weren't on the ride. Good thing when we tossed the eggs over the fence, we kept the cartons. The name of Mario's family market is printed on them. We weren't smart enough to think of that, we were just lucky.

The next morning there is mention of the incident at the roller coaster in the local paper.

"Hey Mario, you made the papers! You're famous!"

He seems to be proud of himself and feels like he has moved up in standing among the guys.

The event is on the lips of many vacationers on the boardwalk near the roller coaster ride which was shut down for a few days. Now, you might think for most kids that stunt would be enough, but not for us. The urge to out-do one another is strong. so something more bizarre has to be thought up. The boardwalk police are still trying to find out who threw the eggs, so we need to be careful.

After a week or two there is a new plot, this one is funny and again we don't want anyone to get hurt so planning is essential. Everyone knows the games on the boardwalk are kind of rigged against the people playing so it's just giving them a taste of their own medicine.

We pick the water pistol game, there are plastic tubes with bull's eyes on them and a small toy monkey sitting on top. The object is to aim your water pistol at the bull's eye and try to fill your tube with water before anyone else. When the monkey hits a plate at the top, a red light goes off and the game is over. The winner gets to pick from a selection of crap stuffed animals.

Our plan, we take up every pistol station and wait for the attendant to hit a switch to start the game. He has a loud speaker attached to a microphone to attract passersby. As he starts his rehearsed speech, a crowd begins to form behind us waiting to see who wins. He announces, "Here we go," and hits the switch. But instead of aiming for the tubes, we all aim for the stuffed animals, the dye from the animals starts to run down the shelves. He is totally stunned; the crowd starts to laugh. The attendant tries to get to the switch to shut the guns off. We start to aim at him instead and as he slips on the wet floor the crowd is getting bigger and bigger which attracts the boardwalk security guards. We can see what is about to happen, so we all drop the pistols and quickly scoot out of the booth. By the time the security guard gets to the game, we are all gone. The crowd tries to explain what happened but everyone is laughing too hard to make much sense.

Again, the next morning the local paper has an article detailing what happened at a boardwalk water pistol game. It sounds more like a comedy skit than a mischievous stunt. The article poses the possibility that the perpetrators might be the same as the roller coaster culprits. The article refers to us as "the boardwalk prank gang".

Some of the guys walk up to the boardwalk during the day to check out the arcade where the game was. There is a sign that says closed for renovation. I guess they have to replace all the wet stuffed animals, which were multi-colored when we left. It really was funny looking back on what happened.

It's been a fun summer so far, I even enjoy working on the construction jobs, learning trades, and earning my own money. My dad is happy that I am doing something worthwhile this summer and my Uncle Nick is proud of the new skills I have with tools.

He always tells me, "If you learn to work with your hands, you'll never starve!

Most of the other guys have part time jobs also so it's hard to get together during the day. But on the weekend, we hang out either on the beach or the boardwalk. One afternoon while we are getting something to eat at the arcade, I notice a ride I never saw before. It's called The Arabian Nights. I tell the guys we should check it out.

So, after we finish our pizza, we walk over and get in line. The boat fits four people but two at a time works better. It's a boat ride through a darkened tunnel with things popping out at you as the boat travels along an underwater rail through a maze. Along the way, you can see several pumps creating a forward movement of the water.

When we get out, we get this great idea, what if we come back tonight when the pier is packed with people and the line for The Arabian Nights is full of young couples. It doesn't matter what the ride is called, it's basically the tunnel of love where couples can make out in the dark and not get caught.

Our plan, we get four plastic bottles of concentrated liquid soap and hide them under our jackets; two to a boat so we will have four boats. When we get to the pumps, we dump all the liquid soap in the water and then wait to see what happens after we get off the ride. We can stand behind the waiting line of people and watch to see if suds come through the swinging doors.

We are laughing already just thinking about what will happen. Off to the super =market to get the soap and meet up at the boardwalk around eight; that is when the boardwalk is most crowded.

It's a warm night so wearing jackets seems a little obvious but it's the only way we can keep the bottles of soap hidden. When we get to the ride, the line is long with couples and some young kids with their parents. Eight guys in line wearing jackets seems a little suspicious but we try to look less obvious by joking around and laughing like it's all fun and games. When it's our turn to get on, the attendant wants to put four of us in one boat, but we tell him we want to ride separately. The line is long, so he is trying to hurry things along and finally lets us go two to a boat.

When we pass through the first set of swinging doors, everything is dark. We can hear the sounds of the riders in the boats ahead as things jump out at them along the way. The first set of pumps is just ahead. Unzippering our jackets, we quickly dump the soap in the water. It lathers up faster than we thought and it's rising in height pretty fast. We yell back at the other guys in the boats behind us to dump the soap now and don't wait until they get to the second set of pumps.

Holy crap, I am freaking out and so are my friends, the soap is moving faster than the boats, if it reaches the end of the ride before we do the attendant will know it was us and keep us there until security show up. What to do, what to do!

I yell back, "Guys, get out of the boats and run toward the exit."

Just picture this, eight kids run out of the tunnel of love through the water, hop over the gate, and down the boardwalk ramp to the street. The people in line are startled and not sure what is happening. The attendant stops taking tickets and loading boats with people to see what the hell is going on. As it turns out, my brother Bill is on the boardwalk with some of his friends and standing close by. He told me later on that when all the commotion started, he had a feeling I must be the cause of it and rushed over to The Arabian Nights to see what was happening.

It looked like gigantic blocks of ice coming through the swinging doors along with boats filled with people covered in suds. Like mountains of white snow, the suds just kept oozing through the doors. They couldn't stop the ride because there were still other boats inside that needed to get out. The boardwalk in front of the ride was covered in soap suds and people were hysterically laughing while younger kids were playing in it!

The security guards are not sure what to do. They turn on the nearby fire hoses to help clean off some of the people and maybe knock down the blocks of suds, but the water spray only makes it worse.

People watching and those trying to help were just shaking their heads and laughing. So were the people covered in soap, I guess they didn't know whether to be mad or happy. It all ended well and nobody got hurt. This definitely was our best prank of the summer.

Again, we made the paper, this time we were on the front page with pictures. The headline reads "The Boardwalk Pranksters Strike Again".

We had one last prank in mind, bring a backpack with water balloons on the ferris wheel and when the car gets to the top, hurl them off onto the people below like a thunderstorm from heaven. But after a little more thought, we felt the likelihood of getting caught was too great. You can't run away from a ferris wheel; quit while you're ahead and maybe save that prank for next season.

My parents would tell their friends who came to visit on weekends all about what was happening in town and showing them the articles in the newspapers covering the stories.

They all would have a good laugh, asking, "Did they ever catch the kids doing all this stuff?"

"Not that I know of," my dad would tell them.

But I would notice my dad and my Uncle Nick looking over at me with a crooked smile.

I would just respond, "Yeah, I heard those stories too. Pretty funny."

The summer is just about over and the stunts we pulled will go down in boardwalk history. Even after fifty years, when you hear some of the older folks talk about the old days in Wildwood, those stories about the boardwalk pranks come up time and time again. I guess that's why my mom cringes whenever she hears a knock at our front door, knowing it's either Alfred or Vinny standing there asking, "Is Bobby home?" My brother Bill now gets a kick out of telling our kids and grandkids about how Bobby and his friends terrorized the boardwalk back in the day!

The ride up was at street level making it easy to stand at the fence and toss eggs into the unsuspecting passengers sitting in the roller coaster cars.

Arabian Nights Water Ride, concentrated liquid soap in the water created a wall of suds to the ceiling of the ride.

SUMMER OF 1962

The water pistol game was always fun, especially when my friends and I took up all the stations and as a prank, when the attendant turned on the game, we just shot streams of water at him and all the stuffed animals hanging from the ceiling and along the back wall. As a side note, the dye on the animals would run down the walls when wet which made the prank even more exciting, however the cops standing behind us were not as amused.

Chapter 12
Time of Your Life Kid!

It's been an amazing summer, one that I will never forget, which is evident by this book, but it's also one that will go down in history, at least as far as boardwalk pranks go.

With the summer behind me, it's time to get ready for high school and a whole new set of rules. It will be an adjustment period for sure, all new kids I won't know and never met. I am sure there will be another orientation process, what a colossal waste of time. For God's sake, the school is so small to begin with, I can find my way to a room with a number that matches my printed schedule. But what the hell, it's a Quaker school, you know, learn to turn the other cheek kind of group. What I learned about turning the other cheek in Catholic School was you did it so the nun could hit both sides of your face. All my friends are going to Bishop Neumann High School, including my brother Bill. I think he performed poorly on the entrance exam on purpose. I, on the other hand am on my way to a Friends' school.

As a favor to my dad, I took the entrance exam along with my brother Bill. Neither one of us wanted to go there but I was the one who got accepted. I didn't have the heart to let him down. Which only goes to prove my motto: "No Good Deed Goes Unpunished".

My dad tells me they still have a dress code; this should be a real hoot! The kids probably look like they stepped out of *Dork Quarterly*. I have no intention of changing what I feel comfortable wearing, I am a product of my home environment. I am an Italian kid from South Philly. We have our standards!

It's only a few days off until school begins, and I watch with disappointment as my neighborhood friends now gather without me talking about starting as freshman at Bishop Neumann. That school is two city blocks wide and just as deep. It's one hundred percent boys most of whom are of Italian descent and all from South Philly neighborhoods so there is kind of a mutual friendship among the incoming class.

I soon found out, that is not the case at Mayflower Central, the school is co-ed with the majority of students from either a Jewish background or Quaker. God, every time I say it, I think of the Oats Cereal, I hate that crap, it tastes like plaster. But there I was like a pair of brown shoes at a black-tie event.

Make the best of it, give it a chance, I am thinking, this school is not cheap to attend, and my dad really wants to give me a leg up in life. I just hope it doesn't turn out to be a leg up to piss on the wall. By the way, this building is well over one hundred years old and smells like mold. But then again, so do the teachers here; they appear to be as old as the building. We are to call the male instructors "Master" and the females, "Teacher". I guess there is a pecking order at Neumann also. I can live with that, it's protocol!

The first few days are spent meeting my classmates and instructors. It's cool so far. I have a class assignment known as Shop. My Uncle Nick would approve, it's a wood working class and there are lots of tools which I am familiar with, including power tools. The students are not allowed to handle power tools without Master Ed's supervision. I am sure I will become the exception to the rule.

After a few days, things begin to settle into a routine. My parents are excited to hear about my new school. I try my best to sound up-beat because I know that is what they want to hear. Not a big problem for me, I learned a long time ago how to bend the truth. It's an acquired skill.

Part of the curriculum is having to sign up for two sports. They don't have a football team, they think it is too rough, so they replaced it with soccer, that figures. I guess they don't have fencing or pistol dueling either! I don't know anything about soccer, but I have to pick something. Golf and tennis are out of the question. At try-outs, the coach evaluates the ability of each player and I have none!

One of the other freshmen is the son of an admiral in the U.S. Navy. He is in command of the Pacific fleet and they are temporarily stationed at the Philadelphia naval yard for refitting some of the ships. The navy yard is only a short distance from where I live on Broad Street. We click as buddies right away. His name is David. He is much taller than I, but mild-mannered and soft spoken. The anti-thesis of myself! I figure it's because of his military family life but we soon become quite good friends and inseparable.

After try-outs, it seems David and I are tagged as fullbacks on the team which is basically the defense. Dave is big and I am aggressive, so we make a pretty good defensive line. Apparently, you're not allowed to use your hands and no tackling. It's not much of a contact sport. It sounds boring, but we have to play a winter sport and this is it!

The season starts off with non-league scrimmage games for practice. Again, Dave and I keep getting these red flags thrown at us on the field. We find out that signifies a personal foul. The coach is constantly yelling at us to play the ball, not the man. Neither Dave nor I get this strategy. If you take out the man, he no longer has the ball, but the coach doesn't see it that way. We are having more fun playing our way than by the rules. Unfortunately, neither Dave nor I manage to finish a game to the end. Another rule, if you get three personal fouls, you are out of the game. We were given the title of the suicide squad! When the official league finally begins, we have one task, determine the best player on the other team and take him out. Make him cautious about driving the ball down field toward our goal, he knew he was going to be a target, even if he didn't have the ball. It worked great for our offensive play. Too bad we could only play the first half of each game before we fouled out. But our team usually won and in our mind that was the main thing. David has a military mindset and I have a street-smart mindset, the objective is and always will be win at all cost, losing is not an option.

We often would ride home together on the local bus; it went right past my house and then directly into the naval base. Many times, I would be invited to the base and hang out with Dave and some of his friends. His family would have me stay for dinner when I was on base. His mom was pleasant, his younger brother was quiet but a funny little kid. His dad on the other hand was totally in command of every conversation, not in a mean way, but spoke with conviction and purpose. I always kept in mind his position in the navy and understood the pecking order. It was fine, just different than the life I lived.

I remember one Saturday afternoon David called to see if I wanted to come to the base and play a game of touch football with some of the kids from the base.

"Sure, what time?"

"How about noon?"

"Ok, sounds like fun." I noticed some inflection in his voice and asked, "What's up Dave?"

"Nothing really, I'll explain when you get here." Then before hanging up, he added, "See if any of your friends want to come as well. Then we can have a team of just us guys against the base kids."

I could tell there was some something brewing with him but didn't press the issue and just said, "Ok, I'll bring four of my friends from the neighborhood."

"Great," he said, "See you then. I'll have my dad leave entry passes at the main gate and meet up with you guys there."

When we get to the main gate, Dave is waiting in a military transport vehicle with a uniformed sailor at the wheel. Dave steps off and comes over for introductions. My friends have never been on the base before and they are awestruck at all the ships, tanks, and artillery, right out in the open. The base also houses the main headquarters for the Marines, so there are lots of guards stationed out front. They don't move, they are like frozen statues keeping watch of everything at the main gate.

Once in the transport truck, I ask "Where are we playing?"

Dave has this strange smile on his face, he leans in toward us all and says, "We are playing on the deck of an aircraft carrier."

We don't say a word, we just sit there with our mouths open.

As the transport travels on toward the docks, Dave gets a little quiet and confides, "I want to kick these guys' asses; they are all jerks. Always a smart-ass comment about my being the son of the admiral and being able to get my way because of him. You met my dad, Bobby; you know it's not like that at all. If anything, it's the total opposite because of who he is."

"I get it, Dave. You would love to rub their faces in it a little and knock that chip off their shoulders." I look at my friends and ask, "What do you think guys? Dave is one of us, let's kick some ass."

They all smile, we are here to win!

The transport truck comes to a stop, holy crap! This ship is huge, you can't even see the end of it.

"Is this where we are playing?"

"Yep, we just have to climb the gangway to the main deck."

When we get there, we just can't believe where we are. Nobody will ever believe this, playing football on an aircraft carrier. Dave walks us over to where the other kids are waiting and makes an attempt at a friendly introduction. There is one kid with whom I can tell Dave has an issue with. I look at my buddies and nod, this is the target. We all smile and start to set up how we are going to play and where the out of bounds lines will be.

"Don't want anyone to fall overboard," comes a snide comment from David's not-so-friendly friend.

"Not to worry buddy," I reply, "we don't play that way. Drowning takes too long. We like immediate results."

The smirk leaves his face as my buddies are laughing.

"Ok, let's play."

The game goes on as it should for a while, it's only two hand touch football. But things take a turn toward a more aggressive kind of play once our team takes a commanding lead.

Dave is our quarterback because he is the tallest among us and can see over the play. Dave takes a cheap hit after throwing the ball. He is not hurt but thrown to the deck by the hit. Ok Dave, this is touch football but that doesn't mean we can't touch really hard, right? The next few plays set a whole new tone, they get it, we are coming hard, and they are about to get squashed. Now we can see blood, it's a hard ship deck and when you hit it, you don't bounce back so easily. The game is finally over and with a team win, we walk over, shake hands, and head down to the mess hall for something to eat. Most of the other kids come with us, but not the kid that Dave wanted to teach a lesson. The other guys seem pretty friendly without the smart-ass kid around. I think the tide has turned in Dave's favor and he won't be dealing with the bullshit any more. It was a great day and a hell of an experience; one I won't forget, and neither will my neighborhood friends.

After we finish eating, Dave arranges for our transport back to the main gate. I hang back a little to thank Dave personally for a great time.

"No," he says, "Thank you. I feel a lot better; don't think I'll be dealing with the bullshit anymore." He puts his hand on my shoulder with the other extended for a firm handshake.

"No problem, Dave, we are friends and friends stick together, no matter what!"

"Can you come for dinner tomorrow night?" he asks,

"Sure Dave, whatever you want."

"Tell your friends I said thanks for coming, it was nice meeting them and helping me resolve some issues. They are welcome anytime, maybe I can set up a tour for them and their parents around the ships and aircraft hangar."

The following night, I show up for dinner and the guards at the main gate by now know who I am, but they still need to check me off their list of names allowed on base. Dave is there to meet me, and we walk back to his place. His mom and brother are there and setting the table for dinner.

"Hello Bobby, make yourself comfortable. Dave's dad will be home soon, and we can all sit for a nice meal. Dave told me you like pasta, so we are having spaghetti and sausage."

"Thanks, you didn't have to do anything special for me, I would be fine with whatever you were having."

"No problem, we wanted to do something different."

I smile and think to myself, *It will be different for sure, everyone in my family makes homemade pasta and sausage, we are Italian after all!* One thing I know for sure is that Italians never order Italian food at a deli. But I appreciate the gesture, I'll put a smile on my face and tell them it's delicious. Like I said earlier, I know how to bend the truth!

Dave's dad walks in and is wearing full military dress. Must have been at a formal military meeting. He greets me with a firm handshake and takes his seat at the head of the table. After saying grace, we all dig in for an Italian meal. Don't laugh, I think his mom did this for me. Dave's dad strikes up a casual conversation about mostly nothing but then it leads into a discussion about the football game on the carrier.

"Oh wow," I say. "That was amazing. Never did that before."

"Well," he continues, "Dave told me about the underlying reason for the game and how you showed up with some of your friends to play ball and make his day. Just wanted to tell you how important it is to have friends you can count on without question. In the military. that characteristic is essential for success. David is lucky to have a friend like you. We, as a family appreciate your friendship. Thanks Bobby, glad you're here."

CHAPTER 13

Where am I Going? What's the Plan?

There is another kid who I am friendly with, really quiet and introverted. I think that was the attraction. My persona seems to always draw me to others who seem to exist on the periphery of high school social life. I did like him though; his name was Mike and with Dave and I as his obvious buddies, no one gave him a hard time.

It wasn't long before my reputation around school was that of a protector. And as Mike told me later on, I was known as one of the cool kids, with a crooked smile I look back at him and reply, not one of, but "the" cool kid.

Mike lived in the opposite end of the city, so hanging out after school or on weekends was difficult. There were occasions when I would invite him to spend the weekend at our house and on others, I would spend the weekend at his. I liked his parents; his mom was very pleasant, and his dad was the head of the procurement department for Philadelphia. Always had a smile when I saw him and always seemed Ok with my being there with Mike.

It's late fall, the school is planning a dance for students on the third Saturday night in October. All the Jewish girls are asking if I was going to be there. I'm not sure, how good is this going to be? A school dance at a private center city Quaker school. What's the theme? What music will they be playing? I doubt if there will be a disc jockey. More likely one of the school faculty putting records of folk music or country music on a small Victrola.

I shake my head and say, "I don't know, I don't think I would fit in with those kids."

"Oh come on, Bobby! You can bring some of your friends and your own records in case we can't dance to what they are playing."

"I don't think the head master would approve of that."

"We can go ask and see what he says."

"OK, I'll meet you girls outside his office after class."

When I show up, there are six of the most popular girls waiting, not for any other reason to mention, but they are all part of the same clique, all Jewish girls from well-to-do families. Alright I think, maybe they have some pull in the school, so let's go find out. We are all sitting in the outer office waiting for Master Larry.

"What can I do for your kids?" he asks, with his hands on his hips.

The girls do all the talking, I am just there for support.

Master Larry looks at me and asks, "What do you have to do with all this?"

"Not much, they wanted me to come to the dance on Saturday night and bring some of my friends."

"Do they go to this school?"

"No, they don't. They go to a Catholic high school where I would have gone."

He pauses for few minutes, turns to the girls, and says, "You all will be responsible for keeping the behavior in line."

The girls seem excited.

Master Larry turns back to me and asks, "Will they be respectful, and will they bring other girls with them?"

The mood changes quickly, they don't want other girls, they just want other boys.

"No," I quickly reply. "It is an all-boy Catholic school."

Smiles again appear on the girls faces.

The leader of the pack asks, "So Master Larry, is it ok for Bobby to bring some of his friends?"

"Yes," he replies, "but no more than ten other boys."

"No problem," I assure him I will stay within the limit.

We leave the head master's office and the girls start asking all sorts of questions about what and who I will bring to the dance.

"Don't worry, Bishop Newmann has a dance every Saturday night and there are literally over one hundred kids there. It will be fine; I'll take care of it."

They have something else in mind, something devious. I think the idea of guys from South Philly being at a Quaker dance is kind of titillating. I am going to ask the guys in my own clique who I trust along with Dave and Mike. Maybe they will learn how to be more comfortable around girls at a dance. One thing is for sure, we can dance and sing and very stylish in our attire. It's what and who all the girls outside South Philly look for at a dance. Not to brag, but in that arena, we totally rule. Other guys hate us for it and it's what usually starts a fight. But at a Quaker school, the likelihood of a fight breaking out with the boys there is kind of funny. I am not too worried about there being trouble. In those circles, it's the girls who call the shots. Watching them trying to control the activity of young Italian guys would be quite the show.

Nonetheless, I am not expecting any problems, we are just showing up to meet and dance. The dance is being held on the second floor of the old gym. When we get there, we are greeted by the head master, who extends a warm welcome to my friends and hopes they have a good time. What he is really saying is, "Don't start any trouble." I can tell he is a little put off by the dress and appearance of my friends, who in fact don't look any different than most inner-city kids at that time.

The girls waste no time introducing themselves and trying to pair off as fast as possible. Walking over to the pilgrim's version of

Dick Clark at Bandstand, I ask if I can spin some of the records we brought with us. He steps back and motions for me to go ahead. My friends are quick to make the first move, grab a girl, and step onto the make shift dance floor, which in reality is the old basketball court. I make sure David and Mike are out there as well by making promises that they can hook up with my guys later on outside in the school yard, in the dark, in private. That seemed to work out well for both my friends and for the horny little Jewish girls.

The night comes to an uneventful close and everyone breathes a sigh of relief. No problems with my friends and the faculty chaperones are pleased. After a little alone time in the school yard, as promised, we are on our way back to South Philly. I arranged for Mike to spend the night at my place so he wouldn't have to take the subway home through North Philadelphia alone late at night. He would be way out of his comfort zone. Dave, of course, lives nearby so he is en route back with us.

Along the way, we decide to stop at Pat's Steaks for a late-night sandwich. It's normal for my friends but a new experience for Dave and Mike. They are trying to understand what this place is all about. The line is around the corner waiting to order and the canopy is covered with photos of famous celebrities who have stopped here for steak sandwiches over the years. It's funny watching them pointing up at the photographs, surprised at the who's who up on the ceiling.

It's a perfect ending to a fun Saturday night. I am glad that my neighborhood friends are getting to know some of the kids from my school, well at least two of them, not to mention the Jewish girls they had the pleasure of making out with in the school yard. I don't know what happened and I don't want to know.

While we are finishing up our sandwiches, Dave mentions that there is a dance scheduled next Saturday night at the base and if we wanted to go, he would arrange for passes at the main gate. Me and the guys are ok with it, sounds like fun. Mike will be away with family but maybe another time for him. Dave tells us the same kids from the football game will be there. The same smart-ass kid thinks he is the best dancer on the base and the girls all want to dance with him.

"Dave," I say, "You're a real crack up. We get it, you want to make him look foolish again. Well, I watched you guys dance, and he is no match for what you guys can do. I would love to knock him down a few more pegs."

Laughing, my buddy Rich says, "How about we knock him off the peg board completely?"

Dave smiles and says, "That would be great."

We shake our heads, swallow the last bit of steak, and start the walk home.

The following week at school is monopolized by Dave's constant talk about the dance coming up on Saturday night. He just wants to be sure we are still coming. Apparently, he has been telling the girls he knows on base that a group of local Italian kids from the neighborhood next to the base are coming to the dance. He tells me they are looking forward to meeting us as well. They watch *Band Stand* and *Soul Train* so they know what kind of dances are popular but not sure how to do them or who they can dance with to learn.

It's finally Saturday night and we are down at the main gate; the guards, as usual, check our names against the list of cleared personnel. Dave shows up again with a transport to take us to what is the equivalent of a dance club.

We walk in and all eyes turn toward us. What we wear is common in our world but a little over the top for military kids. The music is playing but no one is dancing. They are all just standing around drinking soda and eating snacks under the watchful eye of the MPs. Just kidding, some parents are there. It's kind of the same, except at our dances they are called bouncers. Dave asked if we could ask one of the girls he knows to dance, maybe that will get things started. Four of my friends walk over at the same time and ask the girls to dance. That seemed to get things going. After a few records, the dance floor is crowded, and everyone seems to be having a good time.

The smart-ass kid thinks he is cool, so he cuts in on a couple, which is common at dances, but it seems to piss Dave off a little. I tell him not to worry. I walk over to the guy spinning records and give him a few suggestions, some songs are specific to new dances. When he cuts in the new records, most of the dancers stop and walk off the floor, including the kid Dave hates. It's obvious they don't know the latest dance moves, but we do! We now are in charge of the floor. We ask several of the girls to come out, we'll teach them the moves. It doesn't take long for couples to return to the dance floor. All they needed was a little confidence. We are happy to provide that element to the equation. Most of the kids from the base are picking up the moves as well and the atmosphere is happy and friendly.

Except for the one kid, he has been dethroned and is no longer looked up to as the cool kid on base. Dave now has that distinction; his base friends know he has the ability to make things happen. I am happy to have been a part of that transition. I don't know what it's like being the son of a military officer but from what I have seen, it can't be easy growing up like that.

The dance ends on a happy note and we all look forward to doing it again soon. But it's not to be. Back at school the following week, Dave is nowhere to be found. At first, I don't think much about it, maybe he is sick or had other things scheduled that kept him from attending school.

Spring break is coming up next week and my social calendar is filling up quick. That's a joke, at private school they hand you a reading list for books they expect you to finish and write a report on when school gets back in session. I soon find out about Cliff Notes, that is where I focus my attention, I can write a report from those.

I want to spend time with my neighborhood friends from Darien Street and my friends where I live now. I need to catch up on the latest trends and events before I turn into one of the nerds at my school. It is becoming clearer to me and my parents that I am not thriving at the new school. My grades are not spectacular, and I am spending more time in "reflection class" than math class. There is an open house planned at my school once spring break is over and my dad sets up an appointment with the head master to check on my progress.

The night of the open house, I rode with my dad and try to explain why I am not happy at this school. I don't want to tell him about the fights and confrontation occurring on a daily basis because of where I come from and that of my Italian background. I can handle myself there, but if things continue to escalate, somebody is going to get hurt, and it won't be me. I just tell him that I don't belong there, it's not a place I can relate to. Most of the kids are alright but our personalities just don't click.

My dad is listening and trying to understand my position but deep down, he wants me to rise above my peers and have a leg up later in life. I don't want him to think he failed at that.

"Let's see what your head master has to say and we can decide from that point."

I just smile and say, "Ok Pop, let's see where this goes."

The school halls are packed with students and their parents and of course all the teachers and masters. I mingle with some of my classmates and my dad goes off to meet with Master Larry. Dave is there with his dad who is decked out in full military dress; he is an imposing figure.

"Hello Bobby," greeting me with a tap on my shoulder, "Your dad here?"

"Yes, he is in a meeting with the head master."

He just smiles and says, "I don't doubt it!" He continues, "Let me know when he is free. I would like to meet him."

"Will do, sir," I reply. I guess I picked that up from hanging around the naval base.

Dave motions over for me to walk with him down the hall. He wants to tell me something and by the look on his face it appears to be something serious.

"What's up Dave?"

"We just found out that my dad's fleet is shipping out this summer and I won't be here next year. I have no say in the matter, we have no other family here I could stay with, so we are headed back to San Diago as soon as school is over."

I can tell he is holding his emotions in check; I am straining to do the same for his sake. He gives me a hug and we walk back toward the main crowd.

I can see my dad has met up with Dave's father and they are talking in a manner that is not just small talk but looks more intense than just a casual chat. We don't interrupt them and head off toward the refreshments. Mike is there too with his dad who shakes my hand, smiles, and asks where my dad is. I motion over to where he is still talking with the admiral.

He leans down slightly and says, "I want to go say hello. You three stay out of trouble."

Mike looks somber. I guess his dad didn't get great news from his teachers, but neither did Dave or I. So, what else is new?

Dave starts telling Mike about what is happening with him after school ends and Mike is taken back at the news. Dave, Mike, and I have gotten close during the year and losing a close friend when you are a teenager is hard to accept.

I attempt to break the mood with, "Well we still have the rest of this year. So let's make the best of the time we have together."

When the open house ends, we part ways and head back home.

My dad is a little quiet at first but then starts with, "It seems you have made a heck of an impression with Dave and Mike's parents. They have nothing but good things to say about you and how polite and respectful you are when you are at their homes. Dave's father was especially grateful for the impact your friendship with his son has had on his confidence and self-esteem. Mike's dad thinks one day you will be a very successful businessman."

I just sit there smiling and taking in all the new found adulations.

He pauses and then says, "Your head master however has concerns about your adjustment at school. He tells me all your instructors have great things to say about you. You just need to apply yourself a little more and things should fall into place."

"Dad, that's crap. I hate them, and they hate me. This isn't going to end well."

My dad is not pleased with my language or my tone and tells me to stop talking. I need to find my center, knuckle down and finish up the year on a positive note. Exams will be coming soon and if I wanted to stay out of summer school, I would do well to focus more on school and less on my outside interests. I will have all summer to do that. He reiterates for me how much of a sacrifice it is to send me to this private school, and I should keep that in mind.

It was all I could do not to remind him, I didn't ask for this to begin with and I never wanted to go there. I was doing him a favor. Biting my lip, I thought best to keep that kneejerk response to myself. I didn't want to sound like an unappreciative son, but I was out of my comfort zone and out of my element. It's difficult to achieve personal growth under those conditions. I swallow hard and agree to give it another shot.

Summer school though is inevitable. Some of my classes are beyond salvation and the only way I can start fresh in the fall is to bring my grades up this summer.

Believe it or not, the two classes I need to improve are English and French; can that be possible? I need to spend the first five weeks of summer reading and writing in two languages, that sucks. The one saving grace to the entire ordeal was having read a book called *The Catcher in the Rye*. I was so closely connected to the character in the book that I finished reading it in one night.

1963 - Freshman year at Friends Select

Determined not to give into the environment of the new school and maintain my own identity which I struggled to develop in my formative years, I would dress the way my South Philly life style dictated. I was so out of character with the school and its students, it was easy to find the kid you needed to get close to if you were being bullied by upperclassmen. It was also easy for the girls to track me down as well, so there was an upside!

CHAPTER 14

There is a Storm on the Horizon

The summer is going by quickly mostly because the first five weeks were spent in summer school. At least when it was all finished, I was able to improve my grades enough to advance to the next grade.

The remainder of the summer is rather somber, Dave and his family are making preparations for moving back to California. I try to spend as much time with him as possible, but he is busy with family and so am I. We usually head to the seashore on weekends and for two weeks in August. Dave's shove off date is August 17. He will be flying out with his mom and brother; his father will be onboard one of the main ships of the fleet.

I was surprised that his dad made time to meet me one last time before he had to leave, "Take care of yourself Bobby, it was a pleasure getting to know you."

He gives me a quick salute and heads off in a jeep. Dave's mom gives me a hug goodbye and heads back inside. Dave and I just stare at each other, a hug and a handshake seem to take forever, Dave looks down, turns, waves, and walks away. I feel a little empty at having lost a good friend; maybe one day our paths will cross again.

The last few weeks at the shore are quiet, at least for me. I am just not into it right now. I just try not to focus on having to returning to school without my sidekick. But I'll have Mike and one or two other guys to hang with.

Finally, it's time to return to my Quaker prison, trying to remember I promised my dad I would give it another chance. It's all still the same, nothing new except for my schedule. Maybe this year detention, or "reflection" as they call it, won't be a permanent part of my daily routine.

There are a few new kids in my class, they seem alright but it's early yet and you never can judge people from their appearance. Things are moving along without incident. But then something changes. One of the kids in my class comes to me and tells me one of the new kids is a bully and giving others a hard time and taking money.

"So, what do you want from me? No one is giving me a hard time."

"Well," he explains, "they know not to screw with you. You kind of have a reputation in school as a tough guy."

"Who told you that?"

"Everybody knows that," he says. "I would rather pay you than have them take my money."

"Keep your money. I'll go talk to them."

At first, they deny any such harassment but assure me they will leave him alone.

"What about the other kids?" I retort.

Like smartasses, they tell me that's none of my business.

I don't say a word. I just walk away. I have a great idea that will serve two purposes. First, I'll set myself up as the go to guy for protection and secondly, I can make a lot of money selling it. The idea works as planned and I have about thirty kids paying me for protection from any bullying crap. It's just a matter of time before I know a showdown is coming. I get a heads up from one of the clients that they are going to confront me in the field room tomorrow and they are bringing a friend from another school for support.

"Thanks for the information. Not to worry, I got this covered."

Now, I'm an Italian kid from South Philly who grew up protecting myself from first grade. After my last class, I head down to the field room and take away any surprise advantage they may have thought they would have.

Apparently, the word is out because there are kids there from every grade waiting to see what will happen. I just sit on a chair with my feet up on a nearby desk. There is a look of shock on their faces when they walk in and look around. All eyes are on them, and I can tell they are already uncomfortable.

I stand up and ask, "Are you guys looking for me?"

The odd man out says nothing. In fact, he takes a step back. Then comes the inevitable verbal exchange.

"So, you think you are a tough guy protecting everybody from us when it's none of your business?"

I step up almost in their face and say, "It's my business now. At least I don't pick on kids who are alone or smaller than myself just so you can feel like a big man."

It continues. "We know where you come from and who your friends are. We're not afraid of you."

"Well then, that is your first mistake. Why don't you take your friend and leave before you find out you can't leave?"

They make a second mistake, one of them pulls out a pen knife. There comes a gasp from some of the other kids.

"You didn't cut yourself opening that, did you? What is this," I say, "a scene from *West Side Story*?" Bending down, I reach into my Cuban heel boot and pull out an eight-inch switchblade. When it snaps open, it's pretty intimidating. "You sure you want to go there?" I ask.

He quickly puts his little knife away and asks if we could step outside, just the two of us, and work something out.

"Sure," I reply in a calm, low tone, always open to peaceful solutions.

As expected, everything gets resolved, and a white cloud appears once again over this bizarre school.

Unfortunately, that is not the end of this story. It turns out the entire situation gets back to the head master's office, and he wants to see me in his office first thing in the morning. Holy crap, what now? I didn't start any of this shit, I was just drawn into the matter.

I didn't tell my parents anything about what happened. Ignorance is bliss, I thought. Any way. more than likely. it will either resolve itself or explode. Guess I'll find out in the morning.

When I get to school, the halls are a buzz with the recreation of what happened, fact is, nothing happened, but like whispering down the lane, you might think they found a body in my locker. In any event I am on my way to see Master Larry.

When I walk in, there is a strange look on his secretary's face.

"Go in Bobby, he's expecting you."

Opening the office door, he just says, "Sit down. I heard some very disturbing news about you and what happened yesterday. This was a peaceful private school until now, it is not a reform school and violence will not be tolerated. I and the staff have given you every consideration and overlooked many of your antics. We are no longer sure you are suited for this environment."

I can feel tension building up inside and it's just a matter of time before I respond to his bullshit rant. He goes on and on and finally, I stand up and tell him I didn't want to be here either.

"I told my parents that last year, but you kept telling them how well I was doing and how your staff had good things to say about me. I think it was just so you could keep charging my family lots of money in tuition."

By now the secretary has stopped typing in anticipation of what might end up in a fist fight, which I would win against this pompous ass. Instead, I walk out and ask her to call my dad to come get me. The time has finally come for me to leave and head to Bishop

Neumann, where I belong. My dad finally walks in, looks at me, and heads into Master Larry's office. He is not in there long. He comes out alone, I guess Master Ass doesn't want to confront me again. Without a word, we leave the school and head for home.

I tell him the entire story of what happened and how it all ended. I told him I tried to explain it to Master Larry, but his mind was made up in that the entire thing was my fault and my doing.

My dad was calm and listening to me unravel everything I was going through from the beginning. He tells me we are going over to see the pastor of our church and ask him to set up a meeting with the principal of Neumann to get set up there for the rest of the school year. Father McLaughlin is the pastor who picked me for the choir when I was in elementary school. He is more than happy to make a call and write a letter of recommendation for me.

With that in hand, we show up for a meeting at Bishop Neumann. I have my transcript from the Quaker School with my classes and grades. The principal is Father Polini. He is aware of what we want and will do his best to come up with a plan for my attendance.

When I left the Friends School, I was in my sophomore year. However, the classes I had taken would line up with those of a junior here. So, it turns out, I was in an advanced level of study. It makes no sense for me to retake classes I already finished at Friends, but he wasn't prepared to bump me up to a junior level at Neumann. What he came up with was a mixture of classes from each level so I would end up graduating with my age group. My brother Bill is a junior and some of my classes are with his group. With all the class details now worked out, tomorrow will be my first day at Newmann. Finally, Bobby is home!

I know the Catholic school discipline routine, but I am feeling my way through how the system works here and keep up with the allotted time to get from class to class. You don't want to get caught out of class after the bell by the marauding hall monitors.

First day is going well up until lunch. I just follow the guys in my home room down to the cafeteria and sit in the assigned area for my group. I can see my brother on the other side of the room and get up to go over to say hello. He is waving at me to go back. I don't get it, now with the attention of other guys all telling me to go back before you get caught. I kind of freeze in place because I don't get what they are telling me.

Then over the loud speaker comes an ominous call, "You, come here."

I don't realize the message is for me.

Then the voice comes across again, "You, come here."

Dead silence over the cafeteria as I walk up to the raised stand where a priest in a white tunic sits overlooking the entire room.

In my usual wise guy attitude, I am singing, "I am a rock, I am an island."

My brother recalls hearing me and cringing, thinking I'll experience some really harsh treatment.

He slowly comes down to my level and asks, "What's your name? I don't recognize you."

I tell him my name and that this is my first day here. I transferred from another private school. Apparently, he has a reputation for harsh discipline on anyone breaking the rules, so everyone is waiting to see my fate. But none comes. In its place, I am told what the process is for getting lunch and I am to wait until my table number is called. Then, and only then, are we allowed to get up for lunch. I thank him with a smile, which he returns, then I go back to my table.

Everyone is looking at me, asking, "What did he say? Did you get detention?"

Surprised, I ask, "Why? What's the big deal? I told him I was new here and didn't know the correct procedure."

"And?"

"And he told me what it was and to just go back to my table and wait for our homeroom number to be called."

"That's it?" they ask.

"Yes, that's it. Why?"

"Because Father Vandenheuvel is not a friendly priest, I think during the war he was part of the SS."

With a shrug of my shoulders, I just start reading my handbook and wait for our turn at the food counter.

After lunch, I start to make my way to the other classes on my roster, introduce myself, and sit where I am told. At first, I am just in a listening mode. The others have been here for two months already, so they are up to speed with the assignments. I'll find my place in short order and become part of the class.

There is one exception, Father La Luzerne. He is both my math teacher and my mechanical drawing teacher. I felt I had a rapport with him right at the start. Since this was my last class of the day, I asked if I could talk with him after the final bell.

"Sure, I'll be here so just come back to this classroom and we can chat."

We sat and talked for a good long while about a number of things, just getting to know each other. I told him what my future plans were for college and how the curriculum of subjects they gave me left out some of the important mathematics classes I knew I would need on my final transcript to get into the field of architecture and construction technology at Temple University. He explained that he also taught those classes and had room for me if I could make some changes to my roster.

"How do I go about doing that?" I asked.

"Let me work on that with Father Polini and come see me at the end of classes tomorrow."

I felt safe around him, no hidden agenda, not at all like my previous school. I think he just took a liking to me. After all, I was a pleasant kid, well-mannered, soft-spoken, and never in trouble. I had to stop for a moment, make the sign of the cross, and ask for forgiveness in advance. Could this be that proverbial fork in the road I hear so much about? Maybe so, I will find out for sure tomorrow.

With a hand on my shoulder and a smile, we part ways and head for home. Tomorrow will be better, I know more about the school policies and my homeroom priest, Father Frigo, what a character, a jolly kind of priest who speaks with an Italian accent. His family back in Italy are wealthy and own a cheese company that ships product all over the world. He is laid-back and comical. It turns out he is my instructor for the foreign language I have to take this year, and yes, I picked Italian. Go figure!

Your homeroom becomes like your family, all the guys know each other well and hang out in and outside of school. Especially at sports events and school dances. I like the environment I am in now and feel I can grow and prosper here.

At lunch, Father Vandenheuvel catches my eye and waves me over to where he is perched. Again, the cafeteria goes silent, but nothing bad happens, he just wanted to know how I was making out with my new classes.

"Fine Father, thanks for asking."

He tells me, "Last evening at dinner in the rectory, Father La Luzerne was talking to the others about you and how he was impressed at your wanting to get the advance mathematics classes assigned so you would have what you need for your application to Temple University next year."

"Yes," I tell him, "he seemed like he really wanted to help me with that."

"Well, I think you will be pleased with what he managed to get done for you." Then he just smiled and told me to go back to my homeroom table.

My brother, his friend, and my homeroom classmates are dumbfounded.

"What did you do, cast some kind of magic spell over him? He never smiles at lunch, let alone has a casual chat with a student. He is usually inflicting some kind of harsh punishment for even a small infraction."

"I don't know what to tell you. He seems fine to me, I don't know him that well; only met him yesterday."

The guys are looking at me like I am some kind of Shaman.

Lunch is over, classes are over, and I am on my way to see Father La Luzerne about my math classes. Knocking on his classroom door, he motions for me to come in.

"I have good news for you Bobby, I was able to get your roster changed and you are no longer taking the same math classes you took at your previous school, because that would be a waste of time, you now have Geometry, Algebra Two and Calculus One, do you think you can handle those classes all at the same time?"

"I think so."

"Well, I can always help because I teach all those classes."

"When do I make the switch?"

"Starting tomorrow, before homeroom, go to the principal's office and pick up your new roster. Good luck Bobby, I think you'll be fine."

"Thanks so much father, I can't wait to tell my parents. They won't believe how much better things are here."

1964-65
Sophomore at Bishop Neumann High School

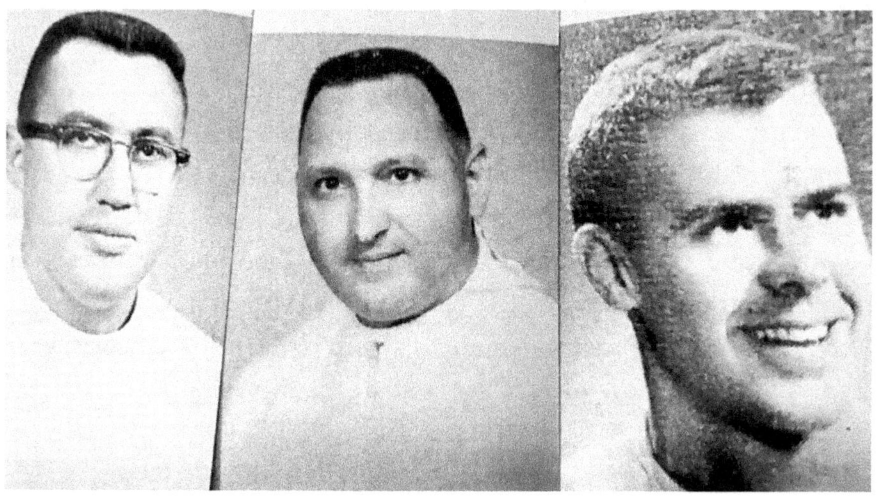

These three priests had the most impact on my transition year from a Quaker School to a Catholic High School.

From left to right: Father Arthur La Luzerne (a mentor, guide, and close friend), Father Martin Frigo (my home room teacher, comic, and purveyor of fine Italian provisions), and Father Augustine Vandenheuvel (disciplinarian, judge, jury, and executioner). However, for me, he was a guide through the maze of rules and regulations.

All three were St. Norbert Priests.

CHAPTER 15
There's a Light Up Ahead

Things are looking up for me. I am in my zone; I have a plan and people around me who are willing to help me get to where I want to be. I have an aptitude for drafting and mathematics, the skills seem to come naturally and Father La Luzerne takes a special interest in what I am doing in class and pushes me toward the harder assignments.

After a while, he lets me help other students who are not quite getting the hang of the drafting tools and the mechanical arm on the table.

He invites me to help with special projects to show off the blueprints from class at the school science fair. We have become good friends. My parents have him over for dinner often and I spend lots of time at the school rectory talking with several of the priest who live there along with Father La Luzerne, mostly about life and ambition.

One day after class, I wanted to go over a drawing I was working on and get his input of how to draw a perspective of a building in three dimensions.

"I can't today, Bobby. I have team practice after school with the varsity soccer team. You can come along if you want. The Soccer field is only around the corner from the school."

"I didn't know you coached soccer. I didn't even know Neumann had a soccer team."

"Why?" he asks. "Do you play?"

"Yes," I answer, "I played fullback for two years at my old school."

"Do you want to play tonight?"

"Sure, but I don't have any equipment here at school."

"Well, I can hook you up with what you need and tomorrow just bring your own gear. Head down to the gym locker room and I'll meet you there so you can suit up."

What a complete turnaround. Now I am trying out for a varsity team that is made up of all Italian guys. Totally different mindset from my last team. This team's mission is to win and win at any price. He introduces me to the guys and pairs me off with Hank, whose real name is Enrico. He is from Italy and played there his entire life. Because of his size, he also plays fullback.

"How do you set up when you play?" he asks.

"Usually I play the man, take him out, strip him of the ball, and pass it over to my partner, that would be you!"

He starts to laugh, "Did they ever have to carry guys off the field when you played?"

"All the time," I smiled back. "Once in a while I even got to play the entire game."

"How come?"

"Because I usually fouled out in the first half."

"Wow," he says. "This is going to be an interesting season. Other schools don't even like playing us, they complain we play too rough. I guess because we turned soccer into a full contact sport."

We high five each other and get ready for a scrimmage in a non-league game.

Father puts Hank and I out on first string.

Running to our position on the field, I ask him, "Do ambulances know how to get to the field?"

He is laughing his butt off as we set up for the flag drop. It doesn't take long for us to pick out their best forward, we hang back and wait for him to make his move down field, toward our goal. Hank motions for me to take the play, charging at their forward full speed, I sweep his legs out from under him and kick the ball over to Hank who sends it back up field to our forwards. Less than five minutes into the game, we are ahead one to nothing. There is a stoppage in play and a whistle for the other teams coach to come on the field. The captain of their team, who I bumped into, is having a hard time catching his breath. Nothing serious, just got the wind knocked out of him.

Hank leans over to me and says, "He's done for today."

The other coach is yelling at the referee and wants a personal foul called against me for a cheap shot. He doesn't get the call, but Father La Luzerne takes me and Hank out for a few shifts just to calm things down.

At the half, Father asks, "Where did you learn to play like that?"

"Prison," I reply.

He is a bit taken aback.

"Just kidding," I tell him. "When I played for my other school, I was on the suicide squad."

He looks over at Hank who is still laughing and gets a stern look from all the coaches.

"Tone it down a little, Bob. This is only pre-season. Everyone is just trying to get into shape for league play in two weeks."

"OK, sorry, it's the only way I know how to play."

"Remember," he says, "it's soccer, not rugby."

We end up winning six-nothing. Needless to say, I am a welcome addition to the team. But the look of concern on Father La Luzerne's face makes me think he is wondering who I really am on the inside. Hope I didn't cause him to lose faith in me. That would suck.

A few days pass, and things seem fine between Father and me.

After the last class, he asks, "Do you want to come over to the rectory tonight after dinner? I wanted to talk to you about something. Nothing to worry about, we can do it another time if you like."

"No, after dinner would be fine."

My dad gives me a ride over and he'll pick me up later when I call home.

My dad is curious, "What did he say he wanted to talk to you about?"

"He didn't say, but it sounded like no big deal." I step out of the car, "I'll call you when we are finished."

Father meets at the front door with a smile and a wave to my dad who is driving away.

"Come on Bob, let's go over to the lounge." He is sitting directly across from me with his hands on his knees and starts, "So, good game the other night. You have some good moves."

"Thanks," I reply, "I try hard."

"Yeah," he interrupts, "maybe a little too hard. I sense a lot of pent-up anger. I never noticed that in you before. It seems to only manifest itself when you are in a competitive situation. Do you feel threatened at times?"

"Not really," pausing for a few seconds, "I feel like I am always being challenged, always having to prove something."

"When did those feelings start?"

"When I was in grade school, I was told I was possessed and evil."

"Who told you that?"

"The nuns."

"Did you ever say anything to the principal or your parents?"

"No Father, you know how that story goes, 'If the nun punished you, you probably deserved it.' So, I just built up these defenses and don't let anyone in, not really in, if you know what I mean."

"I do," he says. "Hopefully now that you told me, you might be able to deal with those issues and let go of them."

"Maybe," I reply. "That would be nice. Thanks for listening."

"I'm not going to discuss anything we talked about with anyone. I'll leave that up to you, whenever you feel the time is right."

"Thanks."

I called my dad to pick me up and while we were waiting, we talked about the league game coming this Saturday.

"I am going to start you and Hank, try not to kill anyone!"

I give him a smirk and ask, "You want to win, don't you?"

"Yes, but tone it down a little."

"Ok, I'll play to the level necessary to win. No more, no less."

"I can live with that," he says and escorts me out to where my dad is waiting. "See you tomorrow."

On the ride home, my dad wanted to know what he wanted to talk to me about.

I told him, "Mostly how I play on the field. He doesn't think I need to be so rough."

"Really? Did you tell him how you ended up in traction at the hospital after one of your games at Friends?"

"No, I didn't want to scare him. He just wants me to tone down my level of play, so no one gets hurt."

"Are you going to take his advice?"

"I'll give it a shot," I say with a smile and a chuckle.

He just shakes his head and says, "One of these days you're going to run into someone just like your Uncle Nick, another hot head."

"I already did," I say.

"Who?" he asks.

"Me!"

"I worry about you, Bobby. You're not as tough as you think you are; there is always going to be someone tougher."

"I know, Pop. I am just playing with you. I will tone it down and be careful. I have priest friends now, and they pray for me. That ought to count for something."

The next morning begins just like any other school day. Father Frigo is in a rare mood and comically interacting with the class. He brought in some cheese from his family's farm in Italy. There is enough for all of us to have a sample. Only Italians can have goat milk mozzarella for breakfast. I raise my hand to get his attention, and in Italian, he asks what is my question.

"Father, did you bring any wine?"

"No, no I can't do that. It's too early."

Never mind that we are not over twenty-one, it's just too early. That's funny. He did bring slices of fresh Italian bread. In Italian homes, wine is like water, so age is of no consideration. We all finish up in time for the first bell. Heading off to our first period still chewing on bread and cheese, I walk past my math class.

Father La Luzerne gives me a friendly wave, "See you later, Bobby," and turns toward a room full of anxious students.

Today I have a short schedule with a free period in the auditorium. The time will be spent thinking about what was discussed last night and the warning from my dad. It's a lot to contemplate but they are serious issues. It's not beyond me, I know I can make the adjustments and channel my energy into a more positive direction. I'm still determined to play to win on Saturday at the final soccer match. With every competitive situation, there has to be a winner and a loser. After all, it is always better to win than lose, as long as you compete fairly. Competition is a part of life. Going along with the flow will relegate you to a level of mediocrity. That's not a good life choice.

You're born, you live, you die, and that's it. Like you were never even here. I would rather be remembered for the crazy things I did in life than not be remembered at all. So much for personal reflection.

Move back to the present, I tell myself.

The rest of the week passes quickly, and tomorrow is the big game. We are having a pep rally by the fieldhouse tonight and it should be epic! A bonfire, cheerleaders, and the school band. This will be a big game; it will determine if we make it to the playoffs. I am only a sophomore but for the seniors this is their farewell event. I know a lot rests on the play of the defense, that means Hank and I, but the night belongs to the entire team and no single player.

The coaches are on a platform and begin to address the crowd. It's a positive and upbeat message. They announce all the players on the varsity team, each one stands up to the cheers and clapping of the crowd as the band plays the school anthem. It will be a high-light of the school year.

Saturday morning is finally here, the team is assembled in the locker room next to the field. You can feel the tension and excitement in the air. The coaches walk in, Father La Luzerne makes a short speech, everyone takes a knee for a team prayer. A loud chant and we are off to the field. The stands are packed on both sides. On the bench, the coaches call out the starters and quickly go over our plan of attack.

After the coin toss, the teams take their respective places on the field. The referee blows the opening whistle and play begins. It's aggressive play for sure and several fouls are called within the first few minutes, but no runs on either goal so far. The first quarter ends without a goal. Our coaches are going over the plan for the second quarter.

Our team captain interjects with his observation of the play so far. "We need to get the ball up field quick so we can play offense. Why are our defensemen holding back?"

The coach tells him they were asked to tone down the play to a less aggressive style.

The captain and several of the seniors chime in, "This is our last chance. We need to play the way we played all season. That's how we got here. We want to win; we will never be here again!"

Everyone is looking at the head coach, Father La Luzerne.

"What say you?" they ask.

He turns to Hank and me and says, "We came to win, so let's win. Bob and Hank," he adds with a smile, "Don't kill anybody."

"Well, there are enough clergymen here for last rights if necessary."

"Not funny guys. Play fair."

Hank and I high five the team and we take the field.

There is a noticeable change in the intensity of play and the referee's take notice. They are watching Hank and I; we have a reputation in the league, nothing un-sportsmen like, just rough play. No one wants to see a player get hurt, but there is physical contact at this level so it's going to happen sometimes.

Hank and I switch to our usual play. Penetration into our defensive zone is all but eliminated. The play is now moving into the opposite team's zone. It only takes a few aggressive plays to bring about a fast break up field and our captain scores first. Within a few minutes, we have a two-goal lead, and it stays that way for the remainder of the game. No one got seriously hurt and we moved into the playoff round.

As it turned out, we didn't win the championship game, but we helped the seniors finish up their final season on a positive note with their heads held high. I am proud of the contribution I made toward making that happen for them.

"Time of your life, kid."

SPORTS

SOCCER WITH MY BISHOP NEUMANN TEAM

Front row third from left: Played three years as fullback for my varsity team, almost never completed a game due to personal fouls early in the match, but I did my best to give my team every advantage by playing the best defense possible. Also spent a good deal of time in the infirmary, but it was worth it!

CHAPTER 16
Getting a Little Freedom

The school year ends on a high note. Next year, I'm a junior and considered an upperclassman. With that comes a junior prom and your class ring. These are big events in the life of a teenager. Mine was no different. There was one more big event that would be happening shortly. My sixteenth birthday and getting a driver's license! That is a game changer, a life altering achievement. The freedom to be able to go wherever you wanted whenever you wanted. Of course, unless you have your own car, there are limitations imposed by the use of the family car.

I will be spending most of the summer season at the Jersey Shore. I have a job lined up with a local home builder and many of my friends will be working at the shore as well. With mobility comes a sense of freedom. I can almost taste it. It's so close and within my grasp. I am not wishing away summer, but I can't apply for a learners permit until August, leaving June and July open for whatever bright idea self-imposed entertainment I could imagine.

Vinny is still my close summer-time buddy, and he hasn't changed much over the last few years. I think living at the seashore all year long, the salt air freezes your brain in the past. Not to mention he is living his life experiences in a much smaller environment than myself.

But I am in his arena for the summer, so I am open to whatever suggestions he comes up with for fun. On the boardwalk, there is an old-time dance hall that once was the home to the most popular big bands and jitterbug music. Now it caters to the sounds of rock-n-roll music being presented by the most popular radio personalities and disc-jockeys of the day. It is called the "Starlight Ballroom"; it is jumping every night of the week. On weekends, however, there is a tremendous influx of high school age kids from all over Philadelphia and other parts of New Jersey. The dance hall gets so crowded they have to put a bouncer at the door to limit how many people can be in the hall at any one time. Vinny is friendly with the DJ and his staff, so we always get in no matter how crowded it gets.

There is one thing I know for sure. The kids from South Philly are always a welcome addition to any dance. They are mostly Italian and always travel in groups, usually by whatever corner they hang on back home. There is always a rivalry between the corners back home, but when they are out of their home turf, all kids from South Philly stick together. We have a reputation of being tough, never out looking for trouble, but somehow there is always a group looking to prove they are tougher. And that is when all hell usually breaks loose. We are also known for how cool we dress and up on the latest styles or making our own style, and, above all, we can dance.

Whenever we showed up at a dance, all the girls wanted to dance with the guys from South Philly. When the dance floor was full, you could feel the boardwalk outside the ballroom bouncing up and down to the beat of the music.

Vinny was the man when it came to getting a corner of the ballroom set aside for my high school friends. Vinny is like a local celebrity and each week he would show up dressed in a bizarre outfit that only he could pull off. The dances were the event of every night. But what about daytime activities? Now that brings me back to my earlier years on Darien Street. The pool hall!

There is a local pool hall in the center of town known as the "Miscue Pool Hall". It was frequented by local fisherman and cadets from the nearby coast guard station. That is until this summer. Each day a swarm of kids from Philly show up and take over all of the twelve pool tables in the place. There are daily challenges to games from the locals and cadets. The Philly kids are better by far and the pool hall becomes our club house. Our guys form a gang and call themselves the "Cross Men" each wearing a Maltese Cross on a chain for identification as a member.

The manager of the pool hall is a colorful character named Morice. He is as gay as they come. Not just a run of the mill gay guy, but a real flamer. He dresses the part and loves entertaining us with song and dance. He becomes our mascot, and we look out for him as well. The pool hall is crowded every day of the week and Morice is doing better than he ever did before. He is happy and we are happy. It's a good partnership.

But like all good things, they eventually come to an end. I just celebrated my sixteenth birthday and applied for my driving learner's permit. I should have it in the mail any day now along with the driving manual from which the test will be given.

When I finally get my permit, I ask my buddy Lou to act as my instructor. We went out driving every day and after only three days, I feel I am ready for my official exam at the DMV. The test is given by a state trooper. They are a no-nonsense group of instructors and there are no second chances if you make a mistake on the driving portion of the test.

The day of the driving test, Lou and I are there early. I pass the written portion of the test perfectly. My name is called by a trooper, and I am escorted to the obstacle course for the driving portion. I pass that test easily and within minutes, I am presented with my junior driver's license.

Wow, a whole new word is opening up that I had not experienced before. My brother Bill and I share access to our family car and my mom's car begins to go through a metamorphosis. We change the components that we feel will give the car more horse power and appeal along the drag strip which is only a few blocks from our house. It's not a legal place to race cars, but on Friday night there are cars there from all over the area, maybe fifty or sixty cars at any one time, racing and showing off until the police appear and break it up. It is a great place to meet girls and get ideas for your own car.

I convince my dad to let me buy my first car, I saw an ad in the paper for a 1958 Chevy Belair for twenty-five dollars. It doesn't run well but it would be great to fix up and rebuild. My dad and I go to check it out and make a deal. We have the car towed to our house and parked out back in our driveway. My buddy Ralph and I figure we can get it back to road worthy with some hard work on our part. Ralph gets a manual for that make and year, and it shows how the car was made and how to repair every component of the drive-train. It's a monumental undertaking but it would be fun to do. We break the entire car down to the frame and our garage floor is covered with hundreds of engine parts.

When my dad sees this, he remarks, "You guys will never get this engine back together."

We make him a deal, if we get it put back together and it runs, he will pay for all the repairs.

He feels it is a safe bet. But in the long run, he is wrong and loses the bet. The car runs great! It looks like crap, but it runs great. It doesn't even have floors and when we drive in the rain, we have to lift up our feet when we go over puddles.

But the satisfaction of having rebuilt the engine and drivetrain is so rewarding and is a boost to our self-confidence. Across from where we live is another friend we call Dippy. He loves the car and wants to buy it. He offers me four hundred and fifty dollars. I accept the deal and use the money to buy another car. My dad can't believe I sold the car for that much money.

"Why did he buy it?" he asks.

"I don't know, he just likes the car. If he changes his mind, I guess he'll sell it to someone else."

My dad shakes his head, laughing, and says, "Where is Dippy going to find another Dippy?!"

Within a few days, my dad tells me a guy he knows who has a mechanic and service station nearby has a car for sale and it looks and runs great. He asks if I want to go with him and check it out. It's literally only a few blocks away.

"Sure, when?" I ask.

"How about now?"

We can walk over to the shop; it's that close. It's a 1959 Ford Fairlane, white with red interior. It looks sweet and he only wants two hundred and fifty dollars for it, that will leave me with two hundred dollars, and I don't need to do much work on it at all. He lets me test drive it home and when I come back, we shake on the deal, and I pay him in cash. Now I have my own car and don't have to share with my brother anymore. It is liberating, to say the least.

The best part is Ralph and I now take turns driving to school, no more public transportation. That is a blessing in itself. Ralph lives across from Lou and the three of us are close friends and do lots of things together. The days of going back to the old neighborhood are fewer and fewer. I don't see Alfred or Butchie much at all. That sucks, but life has a way of changing things around, over which you don't have much control. I could have made more of an effort to see them, even now I have no idea why I didn't.

One day, Lou has an idea he wants to go over with me, he and a buddy Joey, who lives one block over wants to form a singing group. I don't know him well, but we have met several times. Lou and I go over to see him and hear what he has in mind. Joey knows I was in the choir and thinks I would be a great lead singer.

"I think it's a great idea, but we need a fourth singer, any ideas?"

"My friend from where I used to live was in the choir with me. He might want to join us. I can call and ask him."

"Sure, call him, what's his name?"

"Alfred," I tell them.

"Great, call him and ask if he is interested."

I feel really good about having found a way to get re-acquainted with my old friend. Unfortunately, as we get older and our lives take twists and turns, we lose track of both friends and acquaintances, but to lose a childhood best friend with whom you shared so many memories is disheartening.

Reaching out for Alfred was great, we talked about our younger days and all the trouble I got him into. It was like reliving childhood all over again. I explained what precipitated the call in hopes he would be interested in meeting the other guys and see if he wanted to come along.

He answered even before I was finished explaining any details, "I would like that. When do you want to meet?"

"How about Friday night? I could swing by and pick you up about seven?"

"Sure, Bobby, see you then."

Joey had put a few songs together and printed out the lyrics for us to rehearse. We all hit it off great right from the start, it didn't take long to develop a style and harmony.

Joey's uncle was a booking agent and he showed up to listen to us sing. "I like what I hear guys, you keep practicing and put together a repertoire of at least six songs. I can get you booked at several community centers within the next few weeks."

Joey's uncle suggested I be the lead singer because I sounded like Frankie Lymon.

It was a great time for us. We were booked every weekend at a different venue. We dressed alike and had somewhat of a choreography for each song. We had a little fan club and wherever we sang there were always girls' front stage. I never seriously expected to hit the big time, but for kids from South Philly this was a time to remember.

We practiced almost every night. It was customary for guys in a singing group to go around from corner to corner and put on a bit of a show for the neighborhood. If that corner had a singing group, we would have a friendly competition. This happened all over South Philly on Friday nights. During school, groups would get together and sing in the hallways during breaks, it was a fun thing to do, and the priests would stand out in the halls and listen to the acappella version of popular songs.

Neumann had a dance every Saturday night and I, along with my friends and clique, were there every week. Neumann was an all-boys school of about 3,200 students. The girl version of the Catholic high school was Maria Goretti. With an equal number of cute girls, they would be at the dance every week. There were also a number of priests walking around and through the crowd of kids dancing, just to make sure everything stayed morally straight. If you got caught dancing too close with your partner, you would get a tap on your shoulder followed by, "Hey, back off. Leave room for the Holy Ghost."

During the summer months at the Jersey Shore at the dances, I picked up a nickname from some of the girls who were regulars, and I knew well. It was "Bobby Sex", mostly because of the way I danced and because I had a tendency to change the song lyrics to a more provocative version. That name stuck, and whenever the guys or girls I knew saw me at the dance, they would call out, "There's Bobby Sex!"

Even some of the priests called me by that nickname.

The fall semester of my junior year was exhilarating. The months just seemed to fly by. Soon, the holidays would be here and after that, my junior prom. I didn't have a steady girlfriend but that didn't matter, there were plenty of girls I could, and would, ask to the prom. It's early yet and that is not a priority on my list. I am living every day in the present. I don't want to miss a single moment of this year.

WINTER 1965

Typical scene at the Saturday Night Bishop Neumann dance. As usual, there were over two hundred dancers from both Neumann and Maria Goretti high schools. It was at a dance like this, my brother and Kenny came to extract me to come meet his cousin Donna.

SUMMER 1965

My seventeenth birthday at the shore house. My Maltese cross gang affiliation necklace in plain view, my dad and family had no idea what the significance was but at dances and the pool halls everyone knew what it meant.

WILDWOOD BOARDWALK STARLIGHT BALLROOM

This ballroom was a hotspot from the hay days of the big band era, always packed with dancing couples dressed to the nines. During my time in the 1960s, the dance hall still packed with dancers moving to the beat of the latest hits.

Burned down on August 20, 1981 on the Boardwalk, Wildwood, NJ

Chapter 17
Life is What Happens When You Are Busy Making Other Plans

So much has been going on since school started in September. As a junior, there are SATs for college applications, college visitations, and personal interviews with the deans of admissions. Having to get personal letters of recommendation from your high school advisors and lots of posturing to make the best impression possible when a face-to-face meeting is scheduled.

For me, I don't feel the same level of stress as some of my classmates. I have been preparing for this for years. I am focused, committed, and driven. I know exactly what I want to do in life, where I want to go, and what steps were necessary to place me in the perfect position for achieving my goals. Of course, without the help of Fathers' La Luzern and Polini, making sure I was able to take the classes needed to show on my transcript which had to be included in my admissions applications, things would be more difficult. All that remains now is to wait for responses from the colleges.

With my plan in motion, I can spend a little time socializing with friends and classmates as the holiday season quickly approaches. Homecoming weekend is here and the seniors are on track for graduation. For them, senior prom is on the horizon and junior prom is not far behind. Bishop Neumann still holds a dance every Saturday night, now they hold a bit more significance for us, we are upperclassman and looked to for example and advice. I can't help thinking, what crazy kid would want to take advice from me, unless he was planning on a career at a prison camp. Maybe my thinking is a little selfish, I didn't plan for it to be that way, being self-absorbed in reaching my goals was my only focus and priority.

The Thanksgiving Day parade is spectacular as usual and the crowds along Broad Street are in the holiday spirit, friendly and smiling. Young kids on the shoulders of their parents as the floats and bands go by one after the other, all waiting for that one special float that will invoke excitement and uncontrollable joy for the next thirty-five days. The highlight of the parade, the float that has Santa perched at the top of a snow-covered chimney, sitting in a sleigh while motorized reindeer gallop ahead. There is always a large sack of toys propped up behind him as he waves to all the children lined up at the barricades as he makes his way to Gimble's Department Store on Market Street. There to be met by the Philadelphia Fire Department with a ladder truck reaching to the third floor where the toy department is located. Climbing and waving as he makes his way to the open window, there he will step inside, marking the arrival of the official Christmas season. It's a great day for the kids and for Gimble's Department Store.

This year, the holidays seem more special than ever before, although I have no idea why that is true. Maybe it is an omen of good things to come. I always loved Christmas, trying to find the perfect gift for everyone in the family, seeing the look on their faces when they opened a gift they never expected to get. It never mattered what I got as a gift, they were always nice and appreciated but it didn't seem to matter much. You know the saying it's better to give than receive, that was how I really felt at Christmas. Just don't tell anyone, it will ruin my image! The only drawback to those feelings was fostering an inability to show the same excitement I waited to see in others. It was never returned when opening a gift on my end. I never realized that characteristic in myself, but it must have been disappointing. For that, I am sorry. I still have that same issue to this day. I just try to be more aware and show the proper facial response; not fake it, just be more in the moment.

At the time, I was casually dating a girl who lived right down the street. Nothing serious, but fun nonetheless to have someone to go out with on weekends. I knew in my heart that having a serious relationship with a girl from South Philly would be difficult to establish. All the nice girls were somewhat confined to their own circle of close friends or family. So, if you didn't have an opportunity to be introduced by a relative of the girl or be at a family function where a female prospect would be present, the likelihood of you just running into one another was remote. Not to mention it was of immense importance that you meet a nice Italian girl. That's just the way things were at that time. A boy's mother was adamant that any girl you brought home came from a church-going family and could cook. If not, we were told the marriage would not last long.

I never even considered dating one of the girls who hung out on the corner with the guys. Their attributes were specific to survival on the street. They were rough, tough, foul-mouthed when required, and very competitive. Basically, with the obvious exception of biological differences, they were one of the guys. I knew that wouldn't work for me. I never dated, not even casually, a girl from the corner.

It was January of the year 1965, a Saturday night and I was feeling pretty good. I had just officially terminated my steady status with the girl down the street. It wasn't going anywhere; I wasn't even that attracted to her. You know the kind of attraction that makes you want to see that person all the time? We both knew that to be true and parted friends.

I am decked out to make an impression at the dance and exploit my new free status. My parents and brother were going to the graduation party of my dad's good friend Jim's son Kenny, who was more a friend of my brother than of myself. They were the same age. For me, that wasn't a reason enough to miss the weekly dance. They are off and so am I.

At the dance, my friends are all there, both buddies and girls from Goretti. We catch a quick glimpse of each other as I walk in the room to the usual chant, "Hey Bobby Sex over here!"

Father La Luzern came over to say hello and to tell me my pants reminded him of a cheap hotel… no ballroom! He gets a laugh at my expense but that's fine. He is always looking out for me.

The evening moves on, and we are all having a great time. During one of the line dances, I feel a tug on my shoulder followed by hearing my name. When I turn around, it's my brother Bill and Kenny.

I step out of the dance line and ask, "What are you doing here?"

"You need to come with us back to Kenny's party."

"Why?"

Kenny interjects, "You have to come and meet my cousin Donna."

"Again, why?"

"Because we think you would like to meet her."

"I don't think so," I replied. "I just broke up with my girlfriend earlier tonight, I'm not looking for a new girlfriend."

"So what? You have to come. She would like to meet you too."

"How do you know that?"

"Why do you think we are here?"

"Is she conservative or jive?"

"Jive," Billy says, "Come on Bobby, you have to come, the dance is almost over anyway."

Just to clarify, conservative dress is button up shirt with a collar, usually with some sort of oval broach pinned to it, a wraparound madras skirt with a virgin pin to keep it closed and penny loafers.

Jive is tight slacks, usually black with a tight blouse, teased hair, and, above all, desert boots. Those were a must for guys and girls, especially if you were going to a dance.

"Ok, I'll meet you there."

"Don't skip out on us."

"I won't. I need to say good bye to my friends here. Then I'll leave."

I wasn't thinking past the obvious promise of not bailing on Billy and Kenny. Just show up, smile, say hello, maybe have something to eat, meet his cousin Donna, and leave. Now I knew Kenny's parents well, his parents were good friends with mine and they got together often, so I had to be polite when I got there, or my dad would not be happy.

When I walk in, I am immediately greeted by Kenny's dad, Big Jim.

"Bobby, glad you could make it." He puts his arm on my shoulder, it is a really big arm, so I can't break away. "Come over here. I want you to meet my niece, Donna." He calls for her to come over and meet me, neither one of us are pleased with how this embarrassing situation is going thus far. "Donna, this is Bobby, Billy's brother. Bobby, this is Donna. Why don't you go dance?" as he thrusts me out toward her.

The first thing I notice is she is wearing desert boots, that kind of breaks the ice. We, along with others, are dancing. Soon I notice everyone is watching us. I get a big thumbs up from Jim who walks over to tell us he knew we would like each other. Neither Donna nor I comment, we just kept dancing. My plan on leaving was waning with every dance, I wasn't going anywhere. I guess Kenny and Billy were pleased with themselves.

The night is coming to a close and I don't really want to leave. I haven't had an opportunity to really talk with her and that sucked. As everyone is leaving, she walks me out, takes my hand and we smile at each other.

"Are you staying over until tomorrow?"

"Yes," she replies.

"Great, can I see you tomorrow?"

"Yes," she says, "that would be nice."

I didn't dare try to kiss her good night, not with her parents, Kenny's parents, and my parents all watching us say good night.

Once my brother and I were back home getting ready for bed, he asks, "What did you think of Kenny's cousin Donna?"

I kind of stop all motion, think for a moment and without hesitating say, "I think I am going to marry that girl!"

"You're crazy. Go to sleep."

The next morning, I am up early, mostly because I didn't sleep much. I couldn't stop thinking about Donna and what I would say if I saw her again today. Then I get a great idea, I'll ask her if she wants to go to mass with me. That shouldn't raise any eyebrows. How much trouble could we get into at church? I dress quickly and head over to Kenny's house. I muster up the courage to knock on the door. Kenny's mom answers with a smile on her face, knowing already why I am there at 8:45 AM.

"Hello Lena, I was wondering if Donna was here and would like to go to mass with me."

Donna's mom is not so cheery about my being there.

Big Jim walks over and whispers to her, "It's ok, Mary. Bobby comes from a good family, it will be fine. Donna slept over her friend Natalie's. If you could come back in a little while, we'll call over and let her know you were here and coming back to take her to mass."

Leaving for now, I walk back to my car and drive around for about an hour before reappearing at Kenny's house. This time, Donna answers the door and my heart stops. Her entire family is standing behind her watching.

I swallow hard and ask, "Would you like to go to mass with me? It's only around the corner."

She looks back and gets a nod of approval, "Sure, I would like that."

As we walk down to my car, I tell her I was thinking of her all night, she just smiles. I can't recall if she answered me or not, but it doesn't matter. I open the door for her and wait until she is situated before I close the car door. I look up at the house and everyone is at the front door, waving, so I wave back, and we are off to church. I didn't hear one word of the mass, not even the gospel. I was just counting the minutes for the mass to be over.

Neither of us wanted to go back to the house just yet. We still haven't had a chance to talk, not really, how much of a conversation can you have while mass is going on?

"Would you like to go for a ride down to the lakes? It's only a few minutes away but it's a nice park."

There isn't much moving traffic on the roads through the park so it's easy to drive slowly and talk with her. I wasn't expecting this to happen, I kept thinking, *What did I do to have this wonderful girl drop into my life?* I got the impression that she was feeling the same about me. We talked for a long while and not wanting to push my luck with her family, I thought it best to head back to her cousin's house. When we got there, we sat for a few minutes, and I asked if she would like to go out with me next weekend. She said yes with a smile, and I gave her a hug and a kiss.

Then I asked for her number so I could be in touch. We walked back to the house, and I was polite enough to walk her in and say hello to all her family, her dad shook my hand, but her mom looked like she was preparing for an intense interrogation. I thought it best to say good bye and leave. Still smart enough not to kiss her in front of her family. The date was January 31st.

I must have called her every night for the entire week leading up to our date night on Saturday. On Friday evening there is a ring on our phone and my mom answers, I can hear the two-way conversation from where I am sitting, it's Donna.

I hear her ask my mom, "Is Bobby Home?"

I can't help but laugh as my mom hands me the phone. Donna just wanted to say hello and confirm the time I will be picking her up tomorrow night.

It's Saturday morning and I plan on spending the day making my car look like a shiny chariot. I want this night to be special. I don't think my feet touched the ground as I walked to her door to pick her up.

Her dad answered with a smile, Mary, not so much. I get it! Donna is her daughter, and she has a right to be protective. I would be sure not to give her any reason to doubt my intensions. This girl is special and girls like her do not come around in life very often. The odds of meeting your soul mate in life is, at best, very slim, and most never do.

This could be a life altering date. I am not about to screw it up before we even leave the house. Her dad yells up for her, letting her know I am here. I sit with her dad for a brief chat, waiting, then Donna comes down the stairs and I immediately get up to greet her. Wow, I hope they can't hear my heart beating. I take her hand and we say good bye, letting them know we would be home no later than eleven. I still have a junior license and have to be home before midnight.

The night is amazing. I spent most of it just looking at her and smiling. She must think I am crazy, but on the way home, my fears are put to rest when I ask for another date next week, and she says yes. Now I can kiss her good night and this time the kiss tells me she likes me as much as I like her.

But something inside me is churning. I call her every day and night. And on Friday February 5th, I ask her if she would like to go steady with me. She gives me a big hug and kiss, and in that instant, I know for sure what it felt like to be in love. My life has been changed forever. I have no regrets or reservations. She has my heart and I have hers, to cherish, protect and nurture. For I know this is my true love, to have and to hold forever and always. I now know the answer to the question I heard my entire childhood, "Is Bobby home?"

And I can truthfully say to my mother and to myself, "Bobby is home!"

JUNIOR YEAR 1965

Junior prom, now with my steady girl, Donna. Our union was a match that would last a lifetime. I was truly a lucky guy!

Standing with my dad and brother Bruce. With a look of confidence and independence, a big shot in my own mind with a lot to learn in life but for now, I am on my pre-determined path.

Standing with my girlfriend Donna, wearing fashion of the time but never without desert boots. My Aunt Mary looking on, no smile!

1966 - GRADUATION - BISHOP NEUMANN HIGH SCHOOL

Cleaned up and shining like a new dime, I am focused on w here I want to be
and how to get there. Excited, yet well aware that no one is ever sure, what life
has in store. But with Donna by my side, I am up to the challenge!

CHAPTER 18

Conclusion: End of a Childhood Journey

At the age of seventeen, childhood has come full circle. Over a period of twelve years, you tagged along as I journeyed through many wild and sometimes questionable events. You traveled with me, maybe in amazement, as I manipulated situations, I had to face to accomplish whatever crazy scheme was going on at the time. Always managing to convince my friends to help, they and I never seemed to doubt the outcome. There was never a question in my mind as to the success of a plan.

My friends had complete faith in our combined mutual ability to make what looked impossible, possible. We shared in the planning, execution, and accomplishment of the task at hand. I always managed to keep my friends from harm and, when necessary, would take the blame if things went wrong, always wanting to keep my band of accomplices ready and willing to participate in the next bizarre idea.

From an early age my self-confidence was extreme. I didn't like being a kid and always wanted recognition for what I could do. Not because of ego, but for my ability. It was my driving force, always pushing the envelope beyond what was normal.

I wanted to lead, not follow, and my childhood days reflected that ambition. Making money, for me, was a way of gaining respect.

It gave me a sense of independence, although how independent could I have been at such a young age? But in my mind, it did.

Carrying that drive and determination through my formative years was an easy transition. I just kept going, always moving forward, even when I had to go it alone, never thinking twice about the consequences. I knew there would be some but felt I could handle them. I managed to all those times before, so how much worse could they be?

My days of flirting with becoming a priest were short-lived. I guess when I thought I was hearing a calling from above, it was really God saying, "No way, stay where you are. I have my hands full already." So much for the Catholic teaching, "God made us in his image and likeness". It must have been figurative, not literal!

All those events, setting up a neighborhood block party and the punch out cards with the dolls, taught me a great deal about salesmanship, marketing, and follow-through. Those traits pushed me in the direction of wanting to be in charge of my own destiny.

Oh, by the way, the girl I met at her cousin's graduation party, I married her. And in 1968, we began a life together filled with amazing events and experiences. At that time, we were both nineteen years of age. But with her by my side, I knew I could do anything. She was that one piece missing from my life puzzle.

I developed skills and honed my craft. I was an interior designer. I started a contract flooring company, then a general contractor, and finally a successful real estate developer.

The one regret I had was never reaching my goal of becoming an Eagle Scout. The boy scout troop to which I belonged disbanded. I was only able to reached the rank of Life Scout. So, I made a promise to myself that if I had sons, they would become scouts and hopefully reach scouting's highest pinnacle.

I had two sons. They both started out as cub scouts, then webelos, and eventually boy scouts. They both thought being a scout was like being Roman Catholic, you're born into it and you just assume it's the path you are to follow. And follow they did. I was intimately involved in all aspects of their scouting journey. Keeping them motivated and focused. I never forgot what it felt like not being able to complete my journey. That wasn't going to repeat itself. My oldest son Rob achieved the rank of Eagle Scout and shortly thereafter, my son Brian completed his journey and also became an Eagle Scout. No father could be prouder than I was at that moment.

But that isn't the end of the story!

My sons both grew to become fine young men. One became an engineer, the other an attorney. They were blessed with wonderful wives and children of their own. My first grandchild was a beautiful little girl, the only girl in our expanding family tree. I would tell her often, "You are my favorite granddaughter." She also happened to be my only granddaughter. We have a close and special relationship. Whenever she wants something that her parents hesitated about, she would just say, "I'll ask grandpop."

Our family tree expanded yet again with the addition of three grandsons. And like their dads, they were immersed in the scouting life. As each one grew and matured, they followed the journey toward scouting's highest achievement. I participated in their lives on many levels, especially when it came to scouting events. One by one each grandson became an Eagle Scout. Less than one percent of all boys who enter scouting achieve that rank. I am proud to say that I have been blessed to have five boys who can make that claim. I kept the promise I made to myself so many years ago.

The decision to undertake writing this book has been a great experience. I was able to relive the days of my youth and once again feel like I was back in time. It also gave me the opportunity to share with the reader what life for a boy growing up on the streets of South Philly was like. With all its ups, downs, limitations, and temptations, I wouldn't trade it for any other life. In my mind's eye, I can still see each one of my old friends, their faces, the sound of their voices, and their laughs. I can close my eyes and smell Joe's Italian grocery store, the leather from the shoemaker on the corner, the smoke and beer from the pool hall and the Porter House. The smell of a grilled cheese sandwich at Nate's Deli. It's all still there locked in my memory. But life moves on, no matter how hard we try to hold back time.

So, where are all these characters from my childhood, what has become of them?

Alfred moved to Delaware with his parents, I have only had contact with him once since 1970, but I am going to find him. He was too big a part of my childhood to just let him go. But sadly, after much searching, I discovered he passed away in 2015. I waited too long. Alfred, I am so sorry. I love you buddy!

Butchie moved from the neighborhood with his parents in the 60s. But he died an untimely death from an overdose in his twenties.

Harry became a Marine and moved to a seashore town in New Jersey. I found him on Facebook and reached out but haven't heard back.

Frankie became a millionaire by investing in the stock market.

Larry took a job with the VA and has been there for years.

Richard became a professional photographer.

Joey (Parcheesi) Went on to get a job with Parker Brothers. Just kidding, Joey went on to become a priest, I believe he went to serve at a mission in a third world country.

Vinny opened a sandwich shop in a converted railroad box car call Fayha's Two Street Steaks. I never could figure that out, he was not from Philadelphia, and Two Street is primarily an Irish community in South Philly. Then he left to become a taxi driver in West Philadelphia. I lost touch with him in the mid-90s.

Dave went back to the west coast with his family and probably joined the Navy to follow in his father's legacy. I never heard from him again. I always felt sad about that. He was a loyal friend and that is rare.

Mike remained in the area and graduated from the Friends School. I managed to contact him several years ago and had lunch and dinner with him to renew our old friendship. He became a commercial insurance broker and works in center city, Philadelphia.

Lou became a commercial real estate broker

Ralph joined the Marines then became a piano builder and instructor.

Joey became a successful restaurateur.

My brother Billy became a stand in for Flash Gordon. Just kidding, He became a real estate broker and took over our dad's business.

So many others in my memory that I have lost track of over the years but were nonetheless a vital part of my childhood.

As for me, I have gone through many life experiences. Each step adding to my growth and development, adding to my memory bank of happy and sad events. But that is life. It's how you turn those events into a positive and use them to your advantage in the future that really matters.

If someone asked for my advice, which I can't imagine why, I would tell them to go live your life. Don't question your impulses, follow them. If you hesitate, you might just miss out on one of the most amazing experiences that might have come along in your life.

Reach out and grab onto every opportunity, live life. Don't stand on the sidelines and watch life pass you bye. Those moments never come back around. If you can, make mental notes of the highlights. Maybe one day you can recall and share them with your family. It will give them some insight into who you are and how you got to where you are now. Everyone's existence is important, but meaningless if you can't share it with others.

If you take the time to look back on your life as a child, you will begin to understand how every seemingly insignificant event shaped your life. The friends you made, the acquaintances you came in contact with, even if for just a short time, family members, immediate and distant, all had an impact on your life. Things that you hardly took notice of but subconsciously stored in your memory to someday be retrieved, they played a part in your actions and choices along your journey. It all made you who you are.

There are so many people that I wish I could go back and thank. For only now, in retrospect, having known them can be truly appreciated. I don't believe in luck or coincidence, but I do believe in destiny. There is a plan to life. Unfortunately, we don't know what it is until it's upon us.

It is important to remember, especially if you are among my younger readers, that you also have had an impact on others. Everyone you come in contact with will somehow be affected by knowing you. Think about that for a minute, that is an awesome responsibility.

You are either one of your creator's emissaries or you are a quick tap on the delete button for others. Your choice!

I am thankful for my life thus far. I hope you enjoyed reading and traveling with me as I recalled my journey.

Truthfully, I can say at the age of seventy-four, "BOBBY IS HOME!"